START

How to **SUCCEED** when you have **FAILED**

YOUR

VUKANI NXUMALO

IMPOS SIBLE

Published by RedOystor Books
an imprint of RedOystor Media (Pty) Ltd

visit www.redoystor.com for more information
Or contact us at **www.redoystor.com/contact-us**

www.redoystor.com/start-your-impossible
www.facebook.com/VukaniNxumalo
www.twtter.com/VukaniNxumalo

Cover Design & Layout by **RedOystor Media (Pty) Ltd**

Available on Kindle and other retail outlets

ISBN: 978-0-6399789-6-3 (Print)
    978-1-991206-99-2 (Print INT)
    978-0-6399789-7-0 (eBook)

To FAILURE, thank you for the lessons.
To SUCCESS, I look forward to a beautiful journey
with you.

redOystor

London | Johannesburg | New York

DEDICATION

To my sons - Zuzwa and Bandzi

TABLE OF CONTENT

Picture a perfect moment. Hold that image in your mind's eye. Let that be your focus. And with unwavering faith think, plan and act as though SUCCESS is guaranteed.

#StartYourImpossible

PREFACE

Writing a book is not easy, but when you're experienced in what you are writing about, it becomes simple - not easy but simple.

When the idea of writing 'Start Your Impossible' first came to mind, I was down and out. I was licking my wounds from a rather dismal fail in business. I had made many promises and had missed more opportunities than I could recall. And so to speak, I had failed.

My experience with failure has been exciting to say the least. With failure, I have become more enlightened about life and the desire for success.

I've also come to realize the real purpose of life. It is

not about trying to avoid falling over, its about living with full expression even when you do fall over. And that comes with accepting that success is learning from a series of failed experiences and being able to use that experience to launch your impossible.

Experience comes with a certain amount of trial and failure - or is it trial and error. I could be wrong but one of the two should make sense. And I mean the relationship between the two is such that one is not possible without the other.

They say when you hit rock bottom, the only way out is up. Phrased differently, "When you find yourself in a hole, stop digging." I hit rock bottom. I found myself in a deep hole. And when I looked up, I was faced with the grim reminder that failure is not permanent, but also realized that giving up would be the ultimate failure.

Many people have failed before they succeeded. I wouldn't be the first, nor would I be the last. I'm sure the only other reason you picked up this book is because you too are trying to figure out how to succeed when you have failed.

Truth be told, many others have failed and continue to fail. The difference, I have since learned is one's willingness to learn from the lessons that failure seeks to teach and the willingness to try again.

As you are reading this book, you too may be experiencing moments where you are failing. You may also be recovering from a series of failed attempts that did not work out as well as you wanted. Here is a hard lesson you'll have to accept - if you learn from your experiences, you will discover your success. Success is after all a sum of all your experiences – failure and success.

A word of confidence, just because you have failed - once or on a number of occasions, that doesn't make you a failure. A success in the making, maybe. A work in progress, definitely, but not a failure. Believe that, and you have already succeeded. I know it sounds corny from a guy who was bothered enough about his failure, he had to write a book about it. But take it from me, it the corny sounding advice that often makes the most sense.

[WONDERING WHAT IT TAKES TO SUCCEED?]

At the time of writing this book, I was not as successful as I would like to be. Not by a long shot. It could also happen that I've hit another slump and just barely making it. And maybe you are reading this book wondering why in the world would a failed business person like myself write a book about success? Or at least about how to succeed when you have failed.

I have my reasons and will gladly share them with you in the pages that follow. After all, you have spent your hard-earned money to learn how to deal with your own failures or at least turn your failures into lessons of success. William D. Walltles writes in his book 'The Science of Getting Rich' that success begins in the mind. And what the mind can conceive, the mouth will profess, surely the body will take the right actions to bring into form that which was first conceived in the mind.

This book is a documentation of where I have been.

And where I have been is the sum of all my experiences. These experiences have led me to the place where I find myself today - succeeding despite my failures.

This book is also a manifesto of where I am going. And a resolute declaration that whatever failings I may have encountered, by design I was born for success. That not only applies to me, but also to you as you read this book.

If you are willing to learn from your failure, you will surely be successful.

In the pages that follow, you will learn how to succeed when you have failed. Not that failure is a requirement for success, but because many are times when you must fail before you can succeed.

Read well, read carefully. Read between the lines - above the lines and through the lines. The message contained in this book has the power to change the way you see failure. It has the power to propel you into your next level of discovery - self-discovery.

With each word, and possibly with every paragraph, it is my hope that you too will find success by learning from your failures.

INTRO-
DUCTION

Let's get something very clear, you don't have to fail in order to succeed – failure is not a requirement for success. That is not the formula. But ever so often, before we see any kind of success, we fail. Not because we are failures but because we are learning to find our footing in a new experience, an experience that often leads to success.

This book is going to help you understand how to succeed when you have failed. I cannot promise it will be easy, but I believe it is very much possible to succeed even when you have failed. Only if you are willing to learn from your past experiences.

When you are faced with failure, it may be hard to accept that success is possible, but it may also be the only reason you must start your impossible.

As a child when you 'attempted' to walk you must have fallen over a couple of times. It wasn't easy but you kept trying, and finally you got it right. All because you were not afraid to try again.

Each time you got up with a smile and tried again. Your family banded around you with words of encouragement, urging you to give it another shot, screaming 'you can do it' - and you did it.

[IF YOU BELIEVE THESE WORDS, IT TAKES FAILING FIRST.]

You may not have understood a word they were saying, but you could sense their words of encouragement. It was not for you to fail but to drive you to try one more time. At least until you succeeded. And that is the reason you are able to walk today.

Life and business are the same if not similar. The same in the sense that every day is an attempt at something - an attempt at success.

Today, as you experience it, is a new encounter. A new adventure to try out and learn from. After all life is an adventure, enjoy it. And enjoy it to the full.

Every second, minute, hour or day is a fresh experience. It may be similar to the day before because you walked on the same road, took the same route to work or you're sitting at the same cubical as you did the day before. Today, you may have driven the same car or reported to the same old job as yesterday. What remains is, each moment as you live it is a fresh new encounter and a new experience. One you can only account for as a learning adventure. You cannot discount it. Each moment adds to the sum of experiences that make up what you refer to as success.

Well, unless you have resigned yourself to the contentment of what life has to offer, each day is an attempt for a better, brighter and more fulfilling experience - you need to live out that experience for the adventure it is meant to be. An attempt by any other definition is a 'try'. Each day you 'try' to make a better life for yourself and that in itself is success. Or at least success in the making. It is progress. It shows that you want better than what you currently have. And all successful people are like that. Wanting better each day. They wake up each morning with a spark in their eye and a desire to succeed at all costs. Even if that cost comes disguised as failure.

For a good definition of success, remember this – "trying without losing your enthusiasm". You may not succeed all the time, but the more you apply yourself to achieving your goals and dreams, the more successful you will be - all you have to do is 'try".

You were born for success

Before I can tell you why you were born for success, allow me to share with you the story of the one-in-a-million race. It's called one-in-a-million race but the participants who take part in this race do not always add up to a million. Sometimes they are less, most times they are more, however this race is of great importance to the survival of many nations, ideas and generations.

The one-in-a-million race could easily be called a life or death race. Those that cross the finish line - usually one or two but rarely three or more - they become the victors of the day.

The best part is anyone and everyone takes part in the race or has taken part in this race. For as long as you are willing and able, you take part in this race. In fact, whether you like it or not, being alive means you took part in such a race - that might also be the reason why it is called the 'human race'.

Unlike many races you may have taken part in or witnessed, where hours of strenuous training is required to prepare for the race, the one-in-a-million race requires no such preparation – you need only to be ready and willing.

Before a child is born, a million sperm cells must race to the finish line. And the fact that you were born is clear indication that you came out ahead of the pack. If you are a twin, a triplet of any other number other than the only winner, you shared the spoils but that does not make you less of a winner.

Being born was your first of many achievements and should never be your last. Learning to stand and walk was an achievement, learning to read and write, was an achievement. Every action you have attempted and succeeded is testimony to the idea that you were born a success.

Success is ingrained within your DNA. It is a part of who you are. Without it, you would not be reading this book. And because of it, you have to accept my reasoning - success is what we are designed for, but failure is what we must pass through in order to achieve that which we are purposed to achieve.

You may need to fail before you succeed

If you have been down and out, it's easy to believe that maybe, just maybe you are not cut out to achieve the goals and dreams you have set for yourself. At times it may even feel like you are the only one experiencing whatever shortcomings you are going through or have gone through. And that is understandable. I mean when your world is collapsing, it is impossible to see the universe around you.

Many successful people have been where you are, albeit not in the same situation but they have been there. I'm sure they got the t-shirt, but I suspect they sold it to the next generation of would be failures on their way to success. Which is what you will need to do as well - get the proverbial t-shirt and pay it forward.

In 1985, Steve Job, the co-founder of Apple Computers, was fired from his own company. It could not have been easy for him or the person firing him. I can only imagine the day the board of directors called him in to tell him they no longer need his services. He must have had a shock of his life. He started the company for goodness sake. How can they no longer need his services?

It was part of the process he had to go through to become the leader he later grew to be. It couldn't have been easy being laid off from the company you he co-founded. That must have felt like a huge fail. It's hard enough to fail with another person's dreams, how much so when you fail your own.

THE STEPPING STONE TO SUCCESS IS FAILURE.

Fast forward to 2011, Forbes estimated Steve Jobs' net worth to be around $6.5 billion to $7 billion from his sale of Pixar to the Walt Disney Company in 2006.

His success speaks to the reason why this book is necessary. Whatever setbacks you experience, your come back should be better than your last performance - make that one of your bounce back objectives.

After all, it is the lessons we learn from failure that set us up for the amazing successes we are meant to be. Without these lessons we are no better than the last act - learn from failure.

Your success depends on it.

Rumor has it that if Jobs had not sold his Apple shares in 1985, when he left the company he founded for over a decade, his net worth would have been a staggering $36 billion. How is that for a fail turned into success.

Michael Jordan was not picked for his high school basketball team. Six Championships and five MVPs later, Jordan became arguably the greatest basketball player of all time.

If you think about it, if he had given up on his dream, we would not have had the pleasure of enjoying his amazing talent on and off the court.

I can only picture young Michael - being told you didn't make the cut when he had seriously given it his all. It must have been painful not to make it through, but that was probably his defining moment.

This is where he had to decide, "How badly do I want this?" Michael Jordan is often quoted as saying "I have missed more than 9,000 shots in my career. I have lost almost 300 games. On 26 occasions I have been entrusted to take the game winning shot, and I missed. I have failed over and over and over again in my life. And that is why I succeed."

Failure could be your defining moment. A moment of decision. A moment of self-reflection and introspection. A moment when you need to ask yourself – 'How bad do I want this.' Eric Thomas, in The Secret to Success writes 'When you want to succeed as bad as you want to breathe, then you will be successful.' In the midst of all your failings that is what you must ask yourself "How badly do you want it?"

A history of Failed Successes

Before I can tell you how to start your path to success when you have failed, what follows is a documented history of people who failed before they were successful. I suggest you read carefully because success leaves a trail.

Vincent van Gogh only sold ONE painting out of 900 in his life, Red Vineyard at Arles. In a real sense, he was a 'Struggling Artist'.

Lady Gaga got dropped by a major record label after only three months. Apparently, her music was not mainstream enough, and because she was not willing to compromise her style and sound, she got the chop.

Steven Spielberg was denied by USC's prestigious film school not once, but twice. And Oprah Winfrey was fired from Baltimore's WJZ-TV for being too "emotionally involved" with the stories she reported.

This is just the tip of the ice-burg.

When Bill Gates dropped out of Harvard, he started a business with Paul Allen called Traf-O-Data, which flopped. But his passion for computers and his desire to succeed led him to start Microsoft.

It couldn't have been easy starting over, especially from a business where you have previously failed. But together with his partner, they gave it another go, and look where Microsoft is today.

All that Bill and Paul had to do was try again. Their next attempt at business with Microsoft, the software giant as we know it today came to life.

They were carried over and prepared by the mistakes they made with Traf-O-Data. Proving, you see, that while failure is not a requirement for success, you may have to pass through failure on your way to success.

I'm sure it was not easy. Bill and Paul must have had moments when things did not go as well as they wanted, even as they started with Microsoft, but they stuck it out. And that by the way, as you will learn if you dare to finish reading this book, is the only requirement for success when you have failed - sticking it out and seeing your plans through.

Success is not always a straight line between point A and point B. If you follow the trail of many successful people from all around the world, you will notice it has never been a straight line between one point and the next. They faced challenges, they dealt with problems, but they stuck it out.

There will be deviations, there may also be detours and misdirection. But when you want to succeed as much as you want to breathe, nothing will get in your way.

When your desire to succeed is greater than your fear of failure, only then do you have a shot at success.

In fact, let me share with you a couple more stories in detail of how success was born out of many failed attempts.

THOMAS EDISON

In what might be at once the most discouraging statement and worst teaching practice of all time, he was told by his teachers he was 'too stupid to learn anything'. This famous American is attributed with failing over 10,000 times to invent a commercially viable electric light bulb, but he didn't give up.

When asked by a newspaper reporter if he ever felt like a failure and if he should give up, after having gone through over 10,000 failed attempts, Edison simply stated "Why would I feel like a failure? And why would I ever give up? I now know definitely over 10,000 ways an electric light bulb will not work. Success is almost in my grasp."

This is also the same person whose teachers said he was "too stupid to learn anything," and fired from his first two employment positions for not being productive enough. No matter how many times he failed, he kept on trying. And trying. And trying.

Through his many failures, he is documented as the greatest inventor and innovator of all time with 1,093 US patents to his name, along with several others in the UK, and Canada.

At the back of all his failure, Edison refused to give up no matter what. For that, he is credited for his success in the shadow of his failings. So, the question I will pose yet again. How bad do you want it? Do you want it as bad as you want to breathe, because success takes no excuses and demands no apologies?

Henry Ford

Many people know Henry Ford for the Ford Motor Company, one of the most successful automotive companies of all time. However, what many people don't know is that Ford failed twice before, which abruptly resulted in bankruptcies, prior to him successfully launching the present incarnation of his company.

Ford is no stranger to failure, but like Edison, he also didn't give up. Yet, when we think about Ford, we don't picture the failures because all it took was just succeeding one time. Which is true for you as well.

No matter how many times you get it wrong, it takes just one moment to get it right to see yourself through. Sometimes that's all it takes, one deal, one opportunity and when you get it right, your success starts to build up.

Only because you are willing to learn from your failure.

In 1899, at the age of 36 years old, Ford formed his first company, the Detroit Automobile Company with backing from the famed lumber baron, William H. Murphy. That company went bankrupt.

His second attempt was in 1901, when he formed the Henry Ford Company, which he ended up leaving with the rights to his name.

That company was later renamed to the Cadillac Automobile Company. It was Ford's third try, with the Ford Motor Company, that hit the proverbial nail on the head. All because he was never prepared to give up.

We all know the story - at least I would like to think we do. Ford revolutionized the automobile industry, pioneering not only the Model T and the assembly line, but also the concept and notion of an automobile in every home. Driving became a "thing," and subsequently, Ford's Model T went on to sell over 17 million units.

I cannot speak about how he felt or what went through his mind when he was failing one business after another – he is human after all. I'm sure he must have wondered 'Why him', 'Why now', 'What he did wrong or what he did not do right.'

There are many questions that would have flooded his mind. All I can confirm based on the fact that he did not give up, is that in all his wondering, he took a resolute decision to try again. He wanted it bad enough to not give up or let failure stand in the way of his success.

He wanted it bad enough to put aside his feelings and try again - willing to learn from his failure, he was able to start again, and again until he succeeded.

So yes, how bad do you want it? Do you want it as much as you want to breathe?

If yes, you will do whatever it takes to succeed. You may have to fail once, twice or a thousand times over like Thomas Edison, but if your mind is set on success mode and you are passionate about your goals, nothing will stand in your way. I can attest to that, for more than 10 years I carried the dream of our current company.

> # TURN TRIPPING STONES INTO STEPPING STONES.

In many variations, I never lost sight of what the goal was or what the vision looked like.

I kept my eye on the ball and my head in the game.

J.K. ROWLING

Rowling is one of the most inspirational success stories of our time. Many people simply know her as the woman who created Harry Potter. What most people don't know is what she went through prior to reaching stardom. J.K. Rowling's life was not all roses, but it tells a tale of great resilience.

She struggled tremendously. For those who cared to listen, she's told her story many times to inspire college graduates whenever she has been invited to speak. In every one of her speaking engagements she recounts what she went through before she was ever successful.

And when you hear her story you get to appreciate the person she has become. A better version of the original she started with.

In 1990, when Rowling first had the idea for Harry Potter - she says the idea came "fully formed" into her mind one day while she was on a train from Manchester to London.

She began writing furiously. However, later that year, her mother passed away after 10 years of complications from Multiple Sclerosis.

In 1992 she moved to Portugal to teach English where she met a man, married, and had a daughter. In 1993, her marriage ended in divorce and she moved to Edinburgh, Scotland to be closer to her sister. At that time, she had three chapters of Harry Potter in her suitcase.

At no time did Rowling see herself as a failure. She was jobless, divorced, penniless, and with a dependent child but maintained her drive to succeed.

She suffered through bouts of depression, eventually signing up for government assisted welfare. It was a difficult time in her life, but she pushed through the journey. She held onto the only thing that mattered at that time, her child and desire to get published.

In 1995, her script for Harry Potter was rejected by 12 major publishers. It was only a year later when a small publishing house, Bloomsbury, accepted it and extended a very small £1500 advance. A small amount for what she had been through, but it was worth it. It gave her the break she needed.

In 1997, the book was published with only 1000 copies, 500 of which were distributed to libraries. In 1997 and 1998, the book won awards from Nestle Smarties Book Prize and the British Book Award for Children's Book of the Year. After that, it was one wild ride for Rowling.

To date, Rowling has sold more than 400 million copies of her books and is considered to be one of the most successful woman authors in the United Kingdom. Today, Rowling travels around the world speaking about her journey from failure to success.

It cannot be easy being rejected more than 12 times and yet you still have the courage to try again. It cannot be easy believing in something that others see little value on, but you must persist because it may only be your faith that pulls you through.

It is the mustard seed that grows into a big tree. And so, the little faith you possess holds the power to do wonders in your life. Rowling held onto her faith in the work she had started in Harry Potter.

Her faith paid off. And this I want you to know, while you struggle day-in and day-out towards the fulfillment of your hopes and your dreams, know this: "If there is no struggle there is no progress." And progress is the key that opens the doors to your success.

I particularly love the J.K Rowling story because when I started RedOystor Media, I was searching for a publishing company for my first book 'A Different Kind of Thinking.'

Having been rejected over 10 times, I thought why not start my own publishing company.

Using my background in marketing, design and sales, I set off to establish a publishing company with nothing but a dream to see my work in the hands of readers.

Yes, I was not successful at launching and getting my book out, but that desire laid the foundation for why I think our company is positioned to be a game changer in the self-publishing space.

Whatever your vision and goal, it may not be easy, but it will be worth it. You may have to fail a couple of times before you succeed. And I can assure you, if you just keep trying, success is on the horizon.

It may be days, weeks, months or even years before you see any progress. Rest assured, if you keep your eye on the ball and your mind in the game, nothing is impossible. And if you are prepared to work as hard as you can with commitment and determination, you too can start your impossible.

Try? You must. Fail? You might, and if you do, fail fast and fail forward.

Give it your all. And when it seems you are not getting anywhere, do not lose heart, success is usually preceded by many moments that feel like failure. And since you are enjoying reading how you too can turn your failure into success, I think we have room for just one more success that was born out of many failures.

COLONEL SANDERS

People know him because of his iconic white suit and bow tie. Colonel Sanders was the founder of Kentucky Fried Chicken (KFC) - Mr. Finger Licking Good.

With the famous chicken recipe that has dominated the restaurant industry across the world.

Situated at every street corner, and busy district offering a convenient meal on the go. What many don't know is, the zany Sanders got off to a rocky start in life. In fact, it wasn't until the age of 62 that he set out with a $105 social security check in hand that he took on the brave step to pitch his chicken recipe to restaurants. 1,009 people told him he was crazy, but he didn't give up.

Sanders worked many jobs including being a fireman, tire salesman, insurance salesman, and of course, a cook, all just to survive for his idea to thrive. Those odd jobs kept him going.

He brewed up his secret chicken recipe between 1939 and 1940 when he figured out how to pressure fry the chicken in a faster and more consistent than in a frying pan. It was then that he discovered a product that would make KFC world famous. He was at the ripe age of 50 when that happened. It wasn't until 1952 that he hit the road and began trying to sell his franchise model chicken restaurant.

The first restaurant he landed was in Salt Lake City, Utah - USA, which became the first Kentucky Fried Chicken. Amazingly, the restaurant tripled its sales within a year where 75% of their revenue was from the colonel's chicken recipe. The company grew and expanded faster than he could have ever imagined.

In 1964, at the age of 74 years old, Sanders sold the company for $2 million dollars to a group of investors led by Jack C. Massey and John Y. Brown Jr.

He retained the rights to the Canadian franchises and stayed on as a salaried goodwill ambassador to the company. All this goes to show you that it doesn't matter how old you are or how much money you have to your name.

You can do great things if you mind is in the right place. In order to accomplish something great, you need to realize that your desire to succeed is not determined by the size of your pocket nor the date on your birth certificate.

[
GET OUT THERE AND TAKE A RISK.
]

Your desire to succeed cannot be influenced by how old you are. Vision, desire, prosperity have no limits. What you put in is what you get out. When what you want is calling you, the chasing disregards your age and pocket size. You simply set out to go get what you want and with enough persistence you will succeed.

Let me be brutally honest with you. You've failed, that's okay, it's all part of the growing process. We all become better with strife - if we choose to learn from our past experiences. And so what if you have failed, for as long as you are able, you can try again. This I say not to be insensitive, but to give you a perspective of the reality you face.

Lick your fingers - no pun intended, and lick your wounds, yes. You need to. Reflect and find your footing. But giving up is the one option you should never consider because your success depends on your ability to keep your eye on the ball and your head in the game.

If you can do that, no matter how many times you fail, eventually you will be successful. It takes heart to be successful, find that heart.

Let's bring it home

You now know the history of other people who found their success after countless attempts and failures. You might be thinking to yourself – 'But I am not Thomas Edison, or Bill Gates or J.K. Rowling or any of the people mentioned above.'

You are not, you are you. You are no less special than the greatest of them all. You were born and that says you were tasked with something of great value. You too have in you the DNA for success.

That DNA is itching to be explored. You are no less possible than any person that has attempted something great and failed. What they went through you can go through. And when you come out on the other side, you may be just as successful as anyone of the people whose stories I have recounted.

You have great potential, and like a powered battery cell, you need to connect your wiring to see the amazing things you can achieve. The battery cell is a really nothing more than a piece of potential. Connected to the right wiring, you can turn on a TV, run a remote-control car, give light in a torch, all with a small piece of potential.

Within you is massive power to touch and influence the world around you. Understand that failure is not permanent. But when you choose to stop trying, when you don't stick it out, you make failure fatal. It kills your desire to succeed. It kills the vision and talents you are gifted with. It kills you. With a dead vision and desire, starting your impossible, really becomes that - impossible.

If you ask anyone who attended high school with me, they will tell, I would easily make the 'most likely' to succeed list. And here's why, I was an 'A' student for most part of my high schooling.

In fact, in my final year of high school, I received more awards than any other person before me. I made the basketball team with ease. Academically I was at the top of my class. Fellow students and teachers looked up to me so much so that I was voted the head prefect and valedictorian for that year.

If anyone was more likely to succeed, that would be me. The question you might ask, 'Why is the person mostly likely to succeed writing a book about failure?' Good question. I have an answer, but you will not find it on this page. Read on, you've paid for the book, I have every right to keep you in suspense.

Let's get back to the story.

Over the years, my success as it was most likely has been very unlikely to say the least. This is not to say I have failed in every endeavor, but when you think about the things I should have achieved with the kind of potential I displayed in high school, I should be running for president.

Successful as I have been, it's been limited, at least by my standards. With everything I have achieved, I've often found myself back in class – in the School of Life

– learning yet another lesson I had failed to grasp in earlier experiences.

Life being a great teacher, what you do not learn and master or at least find competence in, you will repeat until you are found competent. Sometimes at a very high cost - financially or otherwise.

Money lost, relationships broken, business and partnerships falling apart. It's the price you may have to pay to find yourself. Not because you have lost yourself but because you forgot to connect to your dreams.

This is what one of my mentors had to say about me repeating my failed classes in the school of life, "Once, it's a mistake, twice it's a choice, three times it's a decision." These words are echoed Paulo Coelho '...And a mistake repeated more than once is a decision.' The decisions you make today affect your tomorrow.

I've made many decisions that have cost me dearly, and I'm sure you have too. Otherwise you would not be reading this book.

I have to commend you for making the decision to buy this book by the way. With a title like Start Your Impossible, it couldn't have been easy trying not to look like a loser in the bookstore because the subtitle reads, "How to succeed when you have failed."

Decision? Decisions! Decisions.

With that said, I like to think there is no such thing as a good or bad decision, but only good or bad outcomes. Decision must be made. As best as you can, decisions must be made on the probability that their resulting outcome, at the time of making the decision, will yield a good outcome. That's what successful people do. They make decisions.

You might choose not to make a decision, which is still a decision on its own, and so decisions must be made and are made by default when we choose not to make the decision.

The one decision I made which many successful people have made with fruitful result has to do with my schooling. In my second year of university where I had enrolled for a BCom. Degree in Accounting Sciences, after a rather daunting experience at an audit firm during my vacation work, I decided accounting was not for me.

I did not hate accounting per se, I just did not see myself doing that kind of work for the rest of my life. In fact, if you ask any of my business partners, they will tell you, I am really good at accounting. However, I just don't think I would make a great accountant.

I love accountants, they are very valuable if you want to succeed in business. But for me, that was not the career choice I wanted to follow. The decision was made, I wanted to do Marketing because I came alive in creative spaces. But here I was stuck in Accounting Sciences. And so, I dropped out - technically.

I say technically because I changed course but still stayed in school. Often, I ask myself "Was it a good decision?" Maybe not, but did I make good on the outcome. Yes, I did. On the one hand, I never got to become an Accountant and therefore did not get to drive the fancy German car sooner than my parents would have liked.

The second outcome, I did get to do a Diploma in

Marketing, while I was dropping in for my downgraded BCom Financial Management degree which resulted in the entrepreneur that I am today, I dropped into my passion which was marketing. By anyone's definition, I failed to become an Accountant, and by my definition I succeeded at being an Entrepreneur.

IF YOU DON'T TRY, YOU WILL NEVER KNOW

Some of the wealthiest and possibly the most influential entrepreneurs dropped out of University before they could collect their diplomas – Steve Jobs, Bill Gates and Mark Zuckerberg.

This is in no way a suggestion that dropping out of school or college will result in you becoming a success entrepreneur. Their decision to drop out may seem like a bad decision at face value, but the outcome was positive.

Their path was different, you too need to pick your path and stay the course.

The truth is, if you're ever going to drop out of anything, you better be prepared to drop into something that really fulfills your passion.

Steve Jobs dropped into typography classes, Bill Gates dropped into Business and Mark Zuckerberg dropped into Facebook.

Whatever led to their decision, it wasn't about leaving

school with no plan, they came to the decision because they wanted something better for themselves.

They were answering to a different call. And we are very grateful that they did. The journey was definitely not easy, but it was worth it.

Through many decisions, entrepreneurs around the world have had their fair share of failure. Some resulting in near bankruptcy and others in millions or billion-dollar losses.

A further reason why I believe this book is needed. In fact, it is necessary. Why? Because when you have failed, you need someone or something that will remind you to go back to the drawing board – to refresh your mind, that even when you have failed, you must still strive to succeed.

Someone once said to me, if you ever get tempted to give up, remind yourself 'Why' you started. When you know the 'why', the how and what becomes easy. A lot of people ask what must I do to become successful. Others ask how can I become successful, when the real question is 'Why' do you want to be successful.

It cannot be easy to attempt something when you have failed. I know, I have been there. Each time I've had to remind myself 'Why' I want to succeed.

'Why' I cannot give up. 'Why' I must bounce back when I have failed. I urge you to ask yourself the same question - 'Why?'

Why do you want to be successful? How will being successful impact or change your life? What benefit is there to your success? All these questions will refocus you onto why you want to succeed.

The most successful people in the world are the ones that can answer the question,'Why' and be confident about their desire for success at whatever the cost. Life will knock you down once or twice and if you are lucky, a couple of times.

The reason 'Why' you want to achieve what you want to achieve is what keeps you going. Steve Jobs is quoted as having said, "I want to make a ding on the Universe." He did make his mark. Find your 'Why' and you will make your mark.

Your Success Affirmation

Bouncing back when you have fallen cannot be easy. The road to success is filled with pits and holes. Navigate your way around these pits and holes, and you too will find success.

Like a child who falls each time they try to stand up when they learn to walk, I have discovered that every comeback becomes easier with experience.

My mind has been the source of my strength. This I learned from reading about the law of attraction and the power of the mind from books like 'Think and Grow Rich', 'The Science of Getting Rich' and 'The Secret.'

It is no secret that affirmations work - I call it a conversation with my inner-self. I share this affirmation because it is the spark that flames my every action, it is the driving force behind my passion.

For this reason, I think, if it can light up my fire, I'm sure it can light up yours.

Every morning when I go running and, in the evening, before I go to sleep, I repeat these words to fuel my strength:

I am blessed with financial success and prosperity.

Anything I set my mind to, I do.

I find it easy to make money, because,

I am Happy, I am Wealthy, and I am Prosperous.

And I am successful beyond measure.

You can write and memorize your own affirmation. Make it powerful. It is the inner voice you want to hear in the morning and before you close your eyes to sleep.

Let that be your guiding spark.

1 TO SUCCEED, YOU MUST BE PREPARED TO FAIL

The definition of failure is the 'lack' of success. According to dictionary.com, it is an act or instance of failing or proving unsuccessful.

Yet again, the 'lack' of success.

Can you count the number of times you have lacked success in whatever you've attempted to do? Did you see that as failure or part of the process and journey towards achieving your desired goals?

If you answered with the latter, then this book is definitely for you. Countless success stories are replete with obstacles and mistakes. Some well-intentioned mistakes and others, not. Thomas Edison is said to have failed over ten thousand times before perfecting the electrical light bulb. That did not stop him from trying a different way to get his invention to work.

Oprah Winfrey was fired from her job because she was deemed to be unfit for TV. Her employer at that time told her she gets emotionally attached to the stories she deals with. Who would have thought, making an emotional connection would be the foundation of Oprah's success.

There can be many definitions of what failure may be or mean to you but what must be remembered is, a greater part of what the world sees as failure reflects our true calling to 'Why' we exist. To add value to the world. To touch people's lives and be of influence on a better human race. Or as Steve Jobs calls it, 'to make a ding on the universe.'

Failure resulting from you giving it a go, giving it a try, doing something to push and test the boundaries of your possibilities, should be worthy of praise. Instead we vilify it with words like, shameful, unsuccessful, idiotic and stupid. Instead, failure should be celebrated for the purpose it serves in your life.

Can you imagine Thomas Edison giving up just before the light bulb came on? The world would be a dark place to live in. We might still be surviving by candle light or maybe another inventor might have had a different outcome. Candle lighting would be romantic, but we would have missed a great deal of talent. So, when you have failed not once, twice but more than you can count, it is easy to fall into the trap where you fear failure, not knowing, that is what success is made of.

As Winston Churchill put it, "Success is not final, failure is not fatal. It is the courage to continue that counts." Realize that when you venture into the unknown, you will be met with failure, how you deal with it is the key you your success.

It's understandable why anyone would fear failure, but you shouldn't. Embrace it as part of the process for success. We have defined failure in many words which have resulted in us having a negative perception of what it means to fail.

When people have failed, they have been called anything and everything from unsuccessful, non-performing to downright screw-ups. And none of these words inspire the courage to try again. The only word I actually like there is 'screw up', because, my interpretation is you are 'moving up'.

If you are to succeed when you have failed, your perception of failure needs to change. Screwing up should be something you look forward to - something you embrace. Not intentionally, however recognizing that every screw-up is an opportunity to discover a new way of doing things. A different way of moving up the ladder of success. For this you need a mind shift about your perception and understanding of the true value of failing.

Not as unsuccessful, non-performance or a screw-up but as well-intentioned test of your potential.

Pushing your limits and extending the boundaries of your comfort zone is what you want to do. Outside your comfort zone, that's where the magic happens.

We all want to be successful, but success cannot be guaranteed if you are not prepared to stick it out and screw your way up to the top of your success. That is why your ability to recover from a setback and failure to move forward is essential.

In the top achievers' circles, there is a saying that its crowded at the bottom because everyone is afraid to screw-up and there is room at the top, because successful people are not afraid to screw-up.

Start Your Impossible is your guide to recovery. It is your companion on the journey towards your dreams, goals and aspirations. And you need to know, for you to succeed when you have failed, you will need to embrace your moments of failure just as much as you will celebrate your moments of success. You need to have the tools to process failure and be able to benefit or learn from failure.

Why you should fail before you succeed

As life is a teacher, everything that life puts you through is in preparation for the great things you should accomplish. In fact, your lack of success in the first few attempts should not be a deterrent to venture into the unknown.

The screw-ups we make are what builds our character and the resilience to take on the world in a way that we would otherwise not be able to.

Gain the most from your experience, because as you fail you test your mental strength to withstand the many obstacles that will still come your way.

Like a muscle that must be trained through exercise, you mind needs to be prepared for the journey that lies ahead. It is often said, the greater the adversity the better prepared you will be for your victory. Through your many experiences, you provide your muscle of resilience the kind of training it needs to shoulder your dreams, goals and aspirations.

I know that society has taught you to believe that failure is unacceptable. With that you might have learned that failing means you are not good enough or you did not try hard enough.

Take if from someone who has failed dismally. You can fail. You should fail. I would even go as far as saying you must fail before you can succeed because with failure your readiness for success is enhanced and improved.

This is not to say failure is a requirement for success, but it is a process by which your success gets better and better with each fail. Dales Carnegie says, 'Take a chance, all life is a chance.' And if you don't, opportunity will pass you by. You need to take a chance. Avoiding the possibility of failing by not trying is failing altogether.

If you never try, or take a chance, you can never fail. But if you have not tried you have already failed. What then, is the point of avoiding screwing up, if screwing up is the way you learn to achieve success.

Personally, I would rather screw-up and learn than not try and not discover what could have been a great discovery. Failure is the necessary stepping stone to your success. I call my setbacks 'tripping stones' and these provide the foundation as my stepping stones towards my goals and dreams. Depending on how you look at failure you will either see stepping stones or tripping stones.

Each tripping experience brings you closer to achieving your desires, hopes and dreams – all of which are impossible if you do not try or take a chance. As John Maxwell puts it in his book 'Fail Forward' - be prepared to fail while achieving progress in your journey towards success.

Thomas Edison is famed for saying, 'Many of life's failures are experienced by people who did not realize how close they were to success when they gave up.'

In the same way, every moment where you 'lacked' success, you were one step closer to your success. You tripped, you fell, you got up and stepped up on the very stones that caused you to trip. And so, you must, if not you should fail before you can be successful, because:

ONE: Every time you fail, you become less afraid to fail again.

I remember the first time I tried to play rugby, I was so afraid of being tackled I avoided having the ball passed onto me. I had seen a tackle on TV and it did not look like something I wanted to experience. But when I did finally get the pass, and subsequently tackled, it was not as bad as I thought it would be.

It hurt but not as I had imagined. In fact, when I was no longer afraid of the tackle, I was ready to receive and run, and had a great deal of fun.

Your mind has a way of playing tricks on you, but your mind is controlled by you. The fears you harbor emanate from past experiences where people have told you that failure was not an option - so you avoided failing at all cost. Blinded by this fear, you did not realize that avoiding failure hinders the growth and discovery of your true passions and potential.

Keep this in mind when your mind starts playing 'trick or treat' games on you about the relationship between failure and success; remember this, when you are not afraid, you can conquer the world.

[NOTHING WILL CHANGE UNLESS YOU CHANGE...]

The sooner you fail and learn get to back on your feet, the less fearful you will become. Nelson Mandela said, 'Do not judge me by my successes, judge me by how many times I fell down and got back up again.' And every time you get up, you are less afraid to fall again. Feel the fear and act anyway.

TWO: Failure improves and sharpens your Skills and Abilities.

Truth be told, everyone has failed at something in their lives. In school you showed up with an F, in sports you were greeted with a loss, in life and business you could have faced setbacks and screw-ups.

You may have also failed in marriage or lost a deal to your competitor. Those that tried hard have failed miserably and those that just gave it a shot, they too have failed. And so, failure does not choose its victims or victors. But it rewards those that choose to learn.

What stands out when you fail, your abilities improve. You get better. It's like going to gym. If you have not been to the gym in a while, the first couple of times it's hard to lift the heavy weights.

You may also experience pain the first couple of days. Soon your body gets used to it and before you know it, you are pumping iron like a pro - flexing like you are running for Mr. Universe.

J.K. Rowling, at the lowest point in her life contemplated suicide, not knowing how to provide for her daughter. At that time, she dug deep into her creative source to finish the adventures of Harry Porter. As a result of her setbacks and the rejection by 12 publishing houses, she went on to sell over 400 million copies of books to date. All because her pain had prepared her to take on rejection and adversity with a pinch of salt - if there is ever such a thing.

I found as well, when I had experienced a setback or moment of failure in my life, after a business venture that went south or business relationship that turned sour, that is when I had the best ideas. And this book is one of them.

It is with this experience that I can confidently say, 'We've all failed in one way or another, and guess what, we will continue to fail as we take a chance on life. But we must experience failure because it sharpens our skills and abilities, it forces us to think deep about what we really want and how badly we want it.'

And when you want to succeed as badly as you want to breathe, you will start to see your failure, your setbacks and your screw-ups as nothing more than an opportunity to refine your abilities.

THREE: Failure sets you on a Course Correction.

I've heard that practice makes perfect, I beg to differ. Practice does not make perfect if what you are practicing is wrong.

There is no point climbing the success ladder if the ladder is leaning against the wrong wall. Where are you going? No matter how many times you practice, if what you put to practice is not getting you to your desired destination, you need to change course.

Honestly, there is nothing worse than getting to the top of what you thought would be success only to be told your ladder is leaning against the wrong wall. That's what happens with a lot of people who change careers midlife.

One of my father's friends studied medicine, but discovered he was better suited to business than he was at prescribing drugs and cutting human tissue - he turned what many might see as failure into success by course correcting into a more fulfilling career in business.

He is still a doctor, but a business minded doctor. He is in the business of investing into medical facilities and hospitals - when he realized his ladder was leaning against a wall that did not reflect his desires and aspirations, he took a decision to course correct.

I remember going for a job interview as a Sales Agent for a telecommunications company in Johannesburg, South Africa, all prepared and ready to wow my interviewer with my skills and abilities.

I was there on time, waited in the lobby, and 15 minutes before the start of the interview, I announced myself to the lovely lady at reception only to be told 'Oh no, your interview is at the branch not at head office.'

Needless to say, I didn't get the job, I failed to follow instruction sent to me in an email. In a moment of excitement, I assumed the person whose address was on the email would be the one interviewing me. 'Assuming', the mother of all screw-ups. Call it a blessing in disguise, I have no regrets.

[
SOMETIMES YOU WILL SUCCEED...
]

When you have failed, you are forced to evaluate your course direction. I know because all my life I have known myself to be a creative. This was confirmed in high school when my English teacher gave us an assignment to design an advertisement for spring school. I remember it like it was yesterday, because my soul came alive at the prospect of what I had to deliver - the creative bug bit me right there.

She gave me a mark of 9 and a half out 10. Her logic, I was good, but she did not want me getting it into my head that I was too good for her class. Which reminds me, maybe I should send her a 'thank you' note for discovering my talent for creativity.

Let's get some books sold and she might get more than a 'thank you' note. A successful student is better than a thank you note, right? Sadly, I went on to register for Accounting Science when every fiber of my being was saying I need to be in a creative space. And so I bounced around the system, following what I thought was the ideal career choice instead of following my desired calling.

Interestingly enough each time I have failed in a finance related job, creativity brought me back to life. And so, I like to think failures provide a course correction for where we were meant to be. A reminder of our true calling, if there is such a thing. Though I may not be sure if there is such a thing as a calling, I have learned to listen to the voice of direction.

Evan Williams, in his first company Odeo which was a pod casting platform tried to copy what he thought would be a great business model. To his surprise, he failed, because when Apple announced their pod casting platform Odeo crashed and burned.

Often, we try to copy what we think is a definition of success and we learn the hard way - your success is different.

A hard fail for Williams was a great lesson to learn, helped him find his true passion. It gave him a moment of reflection on the direction his life had to take. Imitation is great, but imagination is so much better. When he decided to try again, he chose a new direction, a different route and approach.

With a renewed focus he took what was gaining popularity at that time - blogging - dumbed it down to 140 characters as micro-blogging and Twitter was born - a true application of his imagination. Because of his initial loss, he had the experience, the knowledge and the courage to sharpen his focus on what he was better at, to create a winning company.

It is a better version of the text message but dumber version of the blog. A simple formula that gets people hooked on Twitter for more than 6 hours of the day.

So, remember, if you fail, and don't find yourself bothered about it, you're walking in the wrong direction. Life has a great tool called failure, used to guide us when we are unsure of where we should be going.

FOUR: Failure reminds you 'why' you started.

In the pleasure of our successes, we may sometimes forget the 'Why'. More specifically 'why' we started, which can lead to a loss focus on what we want, why we want it or even how badly we want it. If what you are doing does not drive you to the point where you are prepared to go the extra mile, you don't want it badly enough.

Working on something we don't care about causes stress. But working on something we love increases passion. A reminder of why you started revives the passion to strive for our dreams and goals - and failure has a way of doing just that. Returning us to the point of first passion.

Often when we lack this sense of drive, we slack and start to 'lack' in success. When you fail because you slack in your efforts, you are challenged to revisit your 'Why!' Why did you apply for the job? Why did you start the business? Why did you register for the course? Why did you get married? Why? Why? Why?

Your experience of failure will get you asking 'why' and the right answers start to emerge. Suddenly you are reminded of why you wake up early in the morning and stay late at night. Or why you are always on time for every meeting. And why you put out your best, always. Failure will remind you why you want to succeed, and how badly you want it. Failure is part of the process and success comes with risks. But when you don't know your 'Why', then you will not push yourself to achieve those dreams and goals.

FIVE: Failure makes you Stronger.

They say what doesn't kill you makes you stronger. No matter how bad your setback may be, if you are not dead, you are much stronger than you were before your experience. By nature, failure is an experience that makes you stronger than you were before. Once you have overcome the obstacles, you pick yourself up and dust yourself off, with courage you take one more chance because you are a lot stronger.

Think of Mike Tyson, if he just woke up some day and decided I want to take on the world champion without the experience of previous punches, he would have been knocked out by the first blow.

The best part about the strength and lessons you learn from failure is that one screw-up teaches you lessons you can use in other areas of your life. A business experience can prove valuable in your personal life. Getting over one obstacle can show you just how capable you are. Embrace that strength and learn from it. Reach deep into this valuable source of strength and make the best of it.

When you learn to be fearless in your personal or social life, it tends to carry over to your professional life.

Think about it, some of the most successful entrepreneurs have a very competitive or fearlessness nature. Richard Branson comes to mind. The activities in his private life create a fearlessness that flows into his professional life.

Similarly, when we pull ourselves up from a horrible breakup, failed marriage or a business that fell apart, the lessons we learn and the strength we develop prepares us for the next challenge. When you do finally face the challenge in a different part of your life, you are a lot stronger than you were before. Your skills, your abilities and strength are enhanced.

With that kind of strength, knowing when to leave a job that is no longer serving you, or starting a business when others have failed becomes an easier decision to make. We gain strength from our failed experiences.

You don't have to fear failure. Embrace it. It is a necessary feature on the road to success. Like the signs on the roads, streets and highway, failure is a guide towards the road which you must take to find success.

. . . And how to deal with failure

Those that have walked the path will tell you, if you want to make it big in the world, fail early, fail fast and fail often. And also remember to fail forward. But when you have failed, the question is, what must happen thereafter?

With the hope that your perception of failure has changed, let's deal with failure and how you can set yourself for ultimate success by facing your challenges head-on with greater skill, strength and ability.

ONE: Embrace it

It's hard when you've been knocked down. It can be painful and humiliating. While small and private fails may be easy to deal with because you alone know about them. Public fails are the hardest do deal with. You may have broken promises, disappointed people who believed in you or fell short of your delivery as a result of your fails.

In order to get back on your feet, you need to embrace your moments of failure. Embrace it with the sense of learning how to do better and different in your next challenge. After all it would be insane to repeat the same thing over and over while expecting a different result.

Before you jump onto the next challenge, fully experience the emotions that come with whatever setbacks you are dealing with. Cry if you must. Scream if you have to. Punch a punching bag if you think that will help you release and embrace your failure. What is key is that you express yourself in a way that helps you embrace your experience.

You may also want to speak to someone you trust - a coach, a professional, or a person with some level of experience in dealing with people and their challenges.

Embrace your feelings – sadness, fear or anger - they are all valid. Without getting overly consumed by these emotions you need to embrace that they are part of the healing process as you prepare to start a new journey. Embracing your emotions and reflecting on the decisions you made that resulted in a failed outcome will help you uncover the lessons you must take into your next adventure.

You need to understand your decision-making process – was it a failure from well-intended error or was it plain carelessness. If it was carelessness, how can you work at making better decisions next time around. When you know these things, you are better able to process your moments of failure with progress and learning. From that you will be able to see the possibilities that failure presents.

Failure will sober you up. It will wake you up to the call of purpose. It will open your eyes to your hidden abilities and skills. And with your eyes open to the different possibilities you can achieve, you will come to realize the impossible is very much possible. Suddenly, your next challenge becomes an adventure as opposed to a scary journey you dare not take.

TWO: Process it

Speeding up and keeping yourself busy can cause you to miss out on vital lessons failure has to teach you. Having embraced the emotions that come with a failed experience, it is important that you process your moments of failure. A process, by design is a system that spews out an outcome of sorts based on the various inputs. It is the answer to the big question, 'So I have failed, THEN WHAT.' Without processing you cannot find the answer to 'Then what.' Where to from here?

In an interview with Brian Koppelman, Seth Godin is said to have suggested, 'Failure is not personal.' You may be personally involved but it is not about you. It's about what you did or did not do that led to your moment of failure.

Understand this, life is a game we must all play. The rules are often created as we go along but the principles are as steadfast as the laws of nature. Gravity doesn't care that you are well educated, rich or stupid, if you step out of a twelve-story building, you will crash to the ground.

In this game of life, you should not take your moments of failure as an indictment that you are now officially a 'FAILURE'. Failure is an event, but you as an individual are not that event and should never be defined by that event.

Successful people fail, they just don't let it define who they are or let it get to them. Take your moments of failure serious, after all they are defining moments in the journey of life, but do not take it personal. It has very little to do with you and everything to do with what you did or did not do right in the process of finding success.

As you process your moment of failure, look at why you failed to understand the things you need to do differently to achieve a better or different result. Did you fail because you did not prepare or was it because you overlooked the necessary processes?

Ask yourself, 'Was it a well-intention error or just plain stupidity?' Was it greed, sloppiness or rushing of things that led to your failure? The answers to these questions will help you understand how you can benefit from your failure. It is a process. I will go as far as saying, get a journal, write down what did not work out the way you intended. Keep record of how you will measure your success against the goals you have set.

In your moment of processing failure, you need to claim the appropriate responsibility for the role you played resulting in the outcome. This is not a chance to pass blame, but an opportunity to reflect on the role you played that resulted in your lack of success.

Taking responsibility is an acceptance that you had a role to play. I repeat, you cannot shift the blame - that serves no one and robs you of a learning experience. And so, you need to acknowledge your role in the situation if you are going to be able to learn from it.

$$\left[\text{... AND MOST TIMES YOU MAY HAVE TO FAIL.} \right]$$

Think about your role in the situation and decide how you will do things differently going forward. Remember the only person you have control over is you - the people, the environment, the circumstances are not in your control. You cannot change the world around you except though influence. But you can change how you act and react through a process of deciding the kind of person you want to become.

Acknowledge your limits if you must - because we all have them. And if there is a need for skills development or a training process you must undergo, seek out the necessary assistance to get better.

Learning doesn't always happen in formal setting, so be prepared to attend seminars, workshops or webinars. However, if needs be, going back into formal academic training should be an option you are prepared to explore. The better skilled, the better prepared you will be.

Success is not an accident, it is only possible when you can learn from your mistakes, process your failure in a manner that allows you to learn and change into the desired outcome to achieve success.

THREE: Benefit from it.

Earlier I said, life is a teacher. Unless you are prepared to learn, you will find yourself moving in circles of one failure after another. You will find yourself digging holes with no idea of how you will get yourself out.

At the end of every processed failure is a benefit, a lesson, a skill and an experience that helps us reach our goals, dreams and aspirations.

The school of life issues not certificates of success. Unlike marriage where you are issued with a certificate before performing well, life puts you through tests and trials with no guarantee of success. You only have your scars and stories as proof of experience.

According to Kentin Waits in a blog post on Wise Bread, failure has its benefits. And if we are to succeed, we must know how to extract the value of such benefits to our advantage because - Failure teaches us lessons. Failure helps us overcome our fears.

Failure reconnects us to our goals, dreams and aspirations. Failure inspires creative solutions. Failure strengthens the core of our values and principles.

Failure evokes the excellence in our purpose. If you are to benefit from the lessons that failure wants to teach you, understand that each of the above benefits are interconnected and not mutually exclusive.

When you have failed, learn the lesson, face your fears, and reconnect with your goals, dream aspirations. It is the only way you will find success. If you ignore any of these benefits you will easily find yourself moving in circles, from one failure to another.

In your moments of reflection - which can also be done with a journal in hand - find creative solutions to the challenges you face because at the core of your values and principles we are designed to be successful. Build on the foundation your experiences have taught you.

Seek out the character within you that will give you the desired results. Keep in mind, as Brian Herbert puts it, "The capacity to learn is a gift; the ability to learn is a skill, however the willingness to learn is a choice." Choose to learn.

With every moment of failure, a better you will emerge. Your purpose will be revealed, and excellence is achieved. Through this book, you have a special gift to learn how to process failure.

Through your experiences you have acquired the skills to learn from the benefits of failure. But ultimately, it is your choice that makes the difference.

At the crossroads of purpose and excellence, there you will find success. It is important that you re-frame your definition of success in relation to failure.

Acknowledging that you will not get things right all the time affords you the opportunity to refocus your energy on working on your success plan. A plan with actions steps that will lead to a success story you can be proud of.

The Power of the Mind

A lot of the times, people give up on trying because they fear failing. And because they fear failure, they begin to think that maybe they don't deserve to be successful - to have that rewarding career, the beautiful marriage or the exciting experiences we often see only in scripted movies.

> MOTIVATION IS WHAT GETS YOU STARTED...

I have a different story to tell you. This story is one you better believe because your success depends on it. Nothing will change unless you change. And if you want to change, your mind has to change. As you have learned, your perception of failure as being shameful needs to change if you are ever going to experience the benefits of learning from it. It is more than a screw-up because it makes you a better person at the end of the day. If you can embrace it and process it, definitely, you can benefit from it.

Seek to express yourself in thoughts and then in word. Think about the kind of life you want to live. The kind of person you want to be.

Reduce your thoughts to paper by writing down who you want to be and what you want in the present sense.

Develop a mantra or an affirmation you can repeat to yourself on a daily basis. It will help you re-frame the conversion that dictates your life's outcome. Think along the lines of 'I am successful beyond measure'. 'I can do anything I set my mind to'. These words will start to filter into your everyday experience.

What you think, ultimately becomes who you are, in your actions and reactions. With these words, you create an environment where you start to see the possibilities of your dreams beyond your failures.

Your success is not only an external attraction but also an internal expression. It is your thoughts that influence your actions, because your thoughts have a bearing on how you feel about your goals and desires.

When your thoughts and feelings are in tune, your desires and actions will follow through.

Very often when you are going through trying times, you need to remind yourself with an affirmation and a conversation with your inner self, as I do every morning and evening with these words:

I am blessed with financial success and prosperity.

Anything I set my mind to, I do.

I find it easy to make money, because,

I am Happy, I am Wealthy, and I am Prosperous.

And I am successful beyond measure.

When your mind is in the right condition; you will start to see progress in how your turn failure into success - very often it begins in the mind. Words don't only express things, they also create things. Words become manifestations, when repeated with faith and emotion -

connecting you to your dreams, goals and vision - these words will drive you to your success.

Thoughts reaffirmed in words have the power to ignite your fire. By reminding your brain to focus on these positive words, repeated over time, they will be impressed upon your subconscious. At a primal level, your physical body will start to act in the manner that responds to your spoken word.

So, when you say, 'Anything I set my mind to, I do.' Your body subconsciously prepares for the commitment to do whatever you set your mind to.

Like prayer, affirmations have worked throughout the ages. Since this book is not necessarily about affirmations, I highly recommend that you read and learn more about them.

REMEMBER! Words create things. Words become things. And words have the power to change your life.

2 | SUCCESS IS A PROCESS

This book is not about failure, this book is about success. If you have not figured that out by now, please read the introduction, you may have missed the part about 'How to SUCCEED when you have failed'

Let's face it, everyone loves a zero to hero kind of story. It makes for good story telling and great reading. And if you look around you, the world is filled with many such people who started with nothing - at least that's what they thought - and worked their way to the top. Personally, I don't think anyone starts with northing. We all have something to offer.

Whether it is your skills, your talents or your personality - there is something about you that makes you valuable. You can't have nothing if you are something. Your creation has everything to do with you being someone or something in this world.

There are many great examples of success stories. People who have overcome obstacles and setbacks to set themselves up for success. People who have sought to achieve their goals, dreams and aspirations.

However, the stories of failure have been known to be far more educational, insightful and inspirational in many ways because they carry the lesson of failure to success.

To give you an example, often sighted are the unicorns of the Internet world - Mark Zuckerberg and Evan William of Facebook and Twitter respectively. Their stories are told in narratives that reference them as amazing creators of innovative ideas. This is not to say Mark and Evan had a smooth ride to the top - in fact they have had their taste of failure. It is their triumph that speaks volume.

I've had my fair share of successes and a decent amount of failure. Some have been private, and others public. Some have cost dollars and cents while others have left my confidence and reputation bruised with millions in lost business. With each one of these experiences, I've come out with some interesting and inspiring revelations.

Granted you will make a mess of things. But if you are to succeed, I say, turn your 'mess' into a message for yourself and others.

My message to you is simple; when you have failed, have the courage to get up and try again. And this time, don't just 'TRY', do what you must do with confidence and conviction in achieving your impossible.

There's no secret. It's a process

If you've ever read 'The Secret' by Rhonda Byrne, you would have come to know about the law of attraction. Simply stated, you manifest what your mind focuses on.

However, it should be noted, whatever manifestation your mind is producing, it is all part of a process.

The farmer that plants his seed cannot expect his crop to start producing immediately. And the farmer knows this. There is a process which his seed must go through for it to germinate and grow into the expected produce. Success is no different.

The highly optimistic farmer may expect 100% production from their planting however the reality is not all seed will germinate and grow into the expected crop or fruit. Likewise, not all your actions will be fruitful. The lack of success in producing fruit from your actions is often referred to a failure.

So, to succeed when you have failed, you need to understand that while failure is not a pre-requirement for success, you may need to fail before you succeed. And when you do fail, don't take it as an indictment on your ability to produce a positive result. All it means is, you may have to try a different approach to achieving your goals.

Most people will agree with me, there is no short

cut to achieving long lasting success. As Warren Buffet is quoted as saying, "You cannot make a baby in one month by getting nine women pregnant."

The secret took care of the law of attraction, 'Start Your Impossible' is not about the law of attraction. My focus in this book speaks to the process you must follow in order to achieve lasting success, especially when you have experienced failure.

In the previous chapter, we spoke about how to deal with failure, so that you get on your way towards success. As a recap, here are the three ways to deal with failure:

ONE: Process it

TWO: Embrace it

THREE: Benefit from it.

All these form part of the journey toward your success. Unless you can process and embrace your short-falls, you can never learn to benefit from the lessons that failure has to teach.

Success is not Linear

When Apollo 11 blasted off into space on July 16, 1969 with Neil Armstrong, Edwin Aldrin and Michael Collins on board, the space craft took a linear direction for only about 5% of the journey. The rest of the way, their success on landing on the moon four days later was guided by many moments of course correction and redirection.

Course correction has a lot to do with moments of failure. When you are faced with a setback in your life, business or career, this may be an opportune moment to reflect on the direction you are headed.

I remember the first time I failed big time, it was one hell of an experience. I was in the process of growing my business and wanted to invite partners who would help me scale and grow the business onto the next level - like any business should.

Without much thinking, I invited friends and family, many of whom had very little experience in business to partner with me. In the heat of excitement, I had contracts drafted and had my new partners added as directors to the company register.

> # ...HABIT IS WHAT KEEPS YOU GOING.

What I failed to realize was, running a company is a lot different to having a party. At a party, when you invite your friends and family over, they are there to have fun. It doesn't matter what experience they have in the fun department. They will take part.

However, in business you need people with experience and commitment to make the relationship work.

The same goes for hiring employees. Experience and commitment are very valuable to your success.

Soon after, when the cracks started to show, I had to adjust and go through a tough and painful course correction – teaching, engaging, mentoring and often having to let go of some people because the relationship was just not working.

It would have been easy to just throw in the towel, give up and just let go of the process. But course correction is not about stopping the car, putting it on park and lying in wait for someone to come and rescue you. Course correct means you may have to turn the wheel, often times you may also have to put on a reverse gear before you can move forward.

As the saying goes, "You may need to take a couple of steps back if you are to make a giant leap." For me this was it. The setback was a couple of steps back, to assess the situation and look at how I can step forward into the future I wanted to create for myself.

'Life is a journey', some anonymous person said that, I didn't. It is with this understanding that you should accept that 'Life is a Journey' and your journey towards your destination will not be linear. It will not be a straight line between point A and point B.

Even if you have never been to space and cannot relate to the story of the first men on the moon, as a person who travels and drives along the many roads, you would know, unless you are prepared to turn the wheel when you hit a road block, you may find yourself driving into walls. And only test dummies are designed to drive into walls.

You may go through long periods where you will not see any results. But that does not mean you have failed.

Like the farmer, the seed may not start germinating immediately after being planted, but that is no indication that the crop will not grow. It must go through a process. Sometimes a painful process of breaking through the ground.

There is something hugely important about success that we all need to realize. When you see no visible signs of progress, remember, it is all part of the process. But when you do come to a point where you are required to course correct, here is how you process failure and redirect for course correction.

How to Process Failure

I hope I am not the first person to tell you this but failing is a reality of life. For many of us, failure helps us grow to become better than we were before we encountered the setbacks we experience.

As has been noted in previous chapters, the greatest achievers – past and present – have from time to time experienced enormous failures; some private and others public. As much as it is all part of life and the process of success, we hate to fail. At least I know I do.

Many times, our failed moments will lead to fear of trying again and sometimes the experience is so traumatic we lose the confidence to give it another go. Our emotions take over, which often means they dictate how we move forward. Before you know it you are locked up in your own cocoon - all because you are afraid to try and you hold back on your journey.

The question you want to ask, as you experience failure is, 'How can you process failure such that it does not lead to stagnation of the process towards success.'

ONE: Don't make it personal.

You might say, 'But I am a person!' How can I not take it 'Personal'?

Remember! Failure is not a definition of who you are. Separate your failed moment from your identity. The two are not the same, they are separate. Just because you have not found a successful way of doing things does not mean you are a failure. You may have failed in that particular instance, but you are not a failure.

$$\left[\; \text{SUCCESS IS ON THE OTHER SIDE OF FAILURE...} \;\right]$$

Thomas Edison is recorded as having tried over 10,000 times while creating the light bulb and yet he failed his way to success. At no point did he see himself as a failure. Besides, taking your lack of success personal hits hard on your confidence and self-esteem.

J.K. Rowling was rejected 12 times when she submitted her manuscript for publishing, during that time she went through some personal tragedies and experiences. She didn't take it personal because deep down she knew all her experiences were part of the process. It wasn't easy but she kept trying.

As Dorothea Brande once said, 'To guarantee success, act as though it were impossible to fail.' JK Rowling went on to sell more than 400 million copies of Harry Porter, inspire a movie trilogy and many other spin-offs. She didn't take it personal. She refused to let rejection and failure define who she is. Against all odds, she achieved greatness - acting as though it were impossible to fail - she guaranteed her success. So can you.

TWO: Assess, Learn and Adapt

The question I always asked whenever I experienced a failing moment is "What did not go right." It's a silly question because the expectation is, you should be asking 'What went wrong?'

Granted, we need to assess that too, but what you want to focus on is 'What did not go right?' This refocuses your mind from wrong to right. Suspend your feelings of anger, frustration, blame and regret and just have an analytical assessment of what did not go right. Was it beyond your control?

How close were you to achieving the expected result? What course adjustment could have been made to achieve a better result? Is there anything different you could have done to achieve a better or different result?

What checks and balance could have been put in place to ensure that you did not land up in the situation you find yourself in?

This assessment is critical to your success because it will provide you with a new learning framework on how to improve and adjust your plans and actions. Later you will learn the importance of planning your actions. Part of this assessment goes back to your plan to compare your plan to reality.

Once you have done your assessment, then you need

to ask, "What can I learn from this?" or "What did I learn from this?"

Thomas Edison is quoted as saying "I didn't fail; I just found 10,000 ways something won't work." He was never discouraged. In fact, for Thomas Edison every attempt was a step closer to success, all because he was able to assess, learn and adapt in the process of finding progress.

THREE: Let Go and Let Live

They say if it doesn't kill you, it will make you stronger. But holding onto the experience of failure will not change the situation.

Very often failure involves other people. People who may have disappointed you and let you down, and you may have also let down and disappointed other people as a result.

I remember in my last experience, there were so many people who were counting on me to lead the success of the project we had started. Things did not go as well as we wanted, and we failed. Yes, we failed.

I remember going for my morning jog and thinking to myself, 'If I don't let go of this, I will be stuck in this moment forever.'

I took a couple of days off to assess 'where we did not go right' and without making it personal, I had to let go and let live. And I started planning how to proceed and progress from there. Every day from then on has been a work in progress to find that sweet spot and drive to make a difference.

Firstly, I congratulated myself for trying; which is important because it recognizes that you have done something right. Then I had a moment of forgiveness, firstly for myself then for the people who may have been involved. Forgiveness is about freeing yourself from the burden of guilt and shame.

At face value it sounded selfish until I was on a flight from Johannesburg to Durban. When making the announcements, the flight attendant said something like, "In an emergency, please place the musk over your face before you try to help others." Then it hit me.

If I was going to keep my promise to myself and the people who trusted and believed in me, I had to be 'Okay'. I had to save me for them. I had to forgive 'me' and them for 'me'. Then prepare to start the impossible.

The mind has a way of playing tricks on us, especially when you hold onto something that is emotionally charged. Holding onto the pain, frustration and regret only prolongs the experience without a solution in sight. And so, the faster you take a positive step forward the quicker you can recover and be on your way to success.

Don Shula, one of the successful NFL coaches in the USA, holding the most successful career wins had a simple policy for his players and staff. The team had 24 hours to celebrate their victories or moan over their defeat.

During this time, the staff and players were encouraged to feel their emotions of success or failure as deeply as they could, however the next day, it was time to put behind all experiences and look forward to the next moment.

I've learned a lot from this philosophy. We live each day as it comes. At the end of each day you assess your experiences and refocus your mind on the next task. Feel the emotions and get in touch with whatever failures you may have experienced. When the 24 hours is up, it is time to focus your energy on the next challenge. If you don't let go, you will not live. You need to let go and let live.

You need to keep your victories into perspective, so congratulate yourself for trying. You need to have a clear understanding of where things did not go right and forgive yourself for failing. Remember, when all is said and done, you need to prepare and ready yourself for the next challenge.

FOUR: Absolve yourself of the need for approval.

It is human nature, when we have done something great; we want our achievement to be recognized. However, when we fail we also seek the approval of those around us to say, 'We recognize you have tried.'

When that recognition and approval does not come, don't beat yourself up about it. Recognize yourself for trying. Take note of your actions because no one else will. Be independent of the need for approval.

A lot of young people choose careers based on the approval of their parents, family and friends. We do the same with relationships and the decision to go into business or not. It's our way of seeking approval. Until seeking approval becomes a form of a drug. The more you take it the harder it is to get off it.

Approval stems from the fear of failure. We want to know the people around us approve of the challenges we take on, so that if and or rather, when we do fail, we can always have collective responsibility for the failure. But it doesn't work that way.

Each person is responsible for their own actions. You may influence others, but you are not responsible for the actions they take.

Have you noticed how people want to be recognized for your success but very few will acknowledge the role they played in any of your failure. It seems, 'in success, we are together, in failure you are on your own.' And you better be able to deal with it.

It's all well to want people to respect you, but you cannot force them. Whether you are right or wrong, successful or unsuccessful, people will always find a way to judge and criticize your actions. So, don't be spooked by what people will say about you.

Besides, if you are ever going to be as successful, you may have to go against the grain. Take the road less traveled or do the uncommon thing - and do it well. To build on your foundation, find your ground. Make your stand and position known to all.

Have solid faith in your dreams and vision for your future. Have that uncanny ability to be your own person even when others seem to think it is not possible. Some people may disapprove of your actions. Others may formulate truths about you based on their own prejudices. Many more will have differing opinions about what you should or should not be doing.

Remember, the only person you should be accountable to, first and foremost, is you. If you give other people the power to influence how you feel about yourself, you may soon find yourself lacking passion and confidence, undermining your ability to achieve success.

Giving other people power over your happiness is like locking yourself up in a jail cell and handing over the key to a person who may or may not be interested in your freedom.

When Robert Kiyosaki approached mainstream publishers for Rich Dad Poor Dad, he was told his book would not sell. The same happened with Zig Ziglar, he too was told his book would not sell. When Michael Jordan was trailing for senior basketball, he was told he was not athletic enough. Oprah Winfrey was told she was unfit for TV.

If any of these people had sought the approval of their 'definers', Robert would have never self-published and become successful as a financial educator, Zig Ziglar would not have become one of the greatest speakers that ever lived.

Michael would have never become the greatest basketball player of all time. And Oprah, oh yes Oprah, she would have never been the greatest face on TV and the first black female billionaire. Take back the control of your happiness.

Successful people are lions, and lions never lose sleep over the opinions of sheep. What people say about you is none of your business. Accept that and move on. Positive or negative, find a way to fuel your fire from within. Affirmations are a great way to start.

You may be worried about your reputation, that is all

good and well. What you need to work on is your char-acter - your ability to withstand that test of time. The good you do will often be forgotten, but who you are, that should never be forgotten.

FIVE: Open your mind to a different view

When Thomas Edison failed, he is reported to have said, 'I have found 10,000 ways why something won't work.' Simply meaning, each time he did not succeed, he tried a different way of doing things.

In the same league as Thomas Edison is Albert Ein-stein, he is recorded as having said, "Insanity is doing the same thing over and over again yet expecting a different result." For things to change something must change. For the results of your actions to turn from failure to success, something needs to change.

Your background and upbringing have a lot to do with who you are today. Your past has influenced the person you have turned out to be thus far. But if the person you are today, no longer serves the purpose to drive your success, something has got to change.

You need a different world view, a different perspec-tive and a different frame of mind. In essence, you need 'a different kind of thinking' - which I wrote about in my earlier book by the same title. Think different about failure. It is not the end of the journey but an opportu-nity to assess, learn and adjust. Think different about what success means to you, it is not a destination but a journey you must travel with adventurous twists and turns. Enjoy the journey without losing focus on the destination.

In thinking different, your perspective and world view will change. Failure will no longer mean you are stupid, weak or incapable. When you understand that every attempt is a step in progress, you will start to see your actions as steps towards success and not setbacks or holdups on your progress.

At every moment, seek to find a positive association to your experiences. See the opportunity to learn and grow. Identify the possibility to achieve your dreams. That is what is hidden in the lessons of your failure.

How to Embrace Failure

By embracing your short comings, you are accepting yourself and your situation as a part of life and the process towards success. In so doing, you are not only giving yourself room to grow; but also, not letting failure define who you are, because your moments of failure are not a measure of your future or self-worth.

Learn to embrace your short-comings, they are the part of you that is key to building your success. Each tripping stone should lay a foundation as a stepping stone. Own your experiences by embracing the lessons contained in failure:

EMBRACE IT: Stop Seeing Failure as a Measure of Self-worth.

The lack of success can often lead to frustration, sadness and regret. Recognize that you are worth more than mere occurrences on your journey towards success.

You are not stupid, you are not dumb, and you are

not incapable. In fact, you making an attempt is cause for celebration.

Many more people have failed because they didn't try. They were stuck at a phase in their life where things did not go right. You trying makes you one up against the odds. You are more than able to bounce back, so while you can feel the emotions, don't be too critical of yourself.

Remember, 'You are successful beyond measure.'

See your self-worth through your ability not inability. Your lack of success in one area of your life does not mean everything you do is a fail. You are not your short-comings.

EMBRACE IT: Focus on what you do well.

In 'The Secret' Rhonda Byrne, explains that the mind does not know negative from positive. What the power of attraction does is put your mind into focus on what you let occupy your mind the most.

To explain this, if I told you to think of a white car, suddenly you will start to notice more white cars on the road. In the same way, when you let you mind focus on your inabilities, more of your inabilities will start to show. So, focus on what you do well.

Use what you do well to your advantage. Let that be your rising point. Whenever I have failed, I lose myself in the service of others. By doing well with others I found that I am able to do well for myself as well. The focus carries over.

Improve what you do well and associate all your actions and results in a positive mind frame. Anytime you find yourself experiencing failure, think of three things that have been positive about the experience. For example, you did not get the job you want, you could think, "I'm glad I got to meet new people." "I'm glad I got to learn something new about myself." "That interview was a great experience, what can I learn from it."

It is these positive thoughts that will energize your next move. By harnessing this energy, you highlight your strengths and abilities, and from there you shift your focus from inability to ability.

EMBRACE IT: Seek Guidance from People you trust.

The worst thing that could happen, stifling your recovery to success, is listening to the right advice from the wrong people.

If you have failed in business, it makes no sense to seek advice from a person who has never been in business and has no experience on how to successfully run a business or even recover from business failure - you want the right people for the right guidance.

Likewise, if you have failed in a relationship, you cannot ask your friend who is also struggling with their relationship to help you fix your relationship challenges. The blind cannot lead the blind.

Find a trusted confidant. If in business, find a successful business person. Ask them, 'Have you failed in business?' If yes, 'How did you work yourself back to success.' The advice they will give you is far much more valuable than the friend who is working a regular job and has never been in business, telling you 'Maybe you need to get a job.'

Keep in mind while the experienced business person has more authority on the advice they give about business, do not dismiss the advice of people who may not be in the field but have experience with your situation - failure is failure. Like I said earlier, the lesson from a personal experience can be just as valuable in your professional life.

It is important that you take advice from people with both the knowledge and experience for the huddle you want to get over. Not all advice is good advice.

EMBRACE IT: Accept your limitation.

No human being comes complete with all the bells and whistles. Some people are better at one thing while others are best at another. You need to know where your limitations are.

You need to know your strengths and your weaknesses. If you are not good with sales, find someone who is better at it than you and partner with them. The most successful people surround themselves with people who complement their shortcomings.

If you are not great at finances and accounting, get the help you need - someone more capable. And if you can't find help at that given moment, make an effort to reduce your limitations by learning the required skills and competences.

Hopefully you will never have to outsource any of your limitations in a relationship, it is not a recommendation I would make. Whatever your limitations, you can make up for them in another area of your life.

Also remember, the only person you have control over is you, and no one else. Learn to accept the things you cannot change and change the things you cannot accept - it's really that simple. Focus on your strengths, and your weakness will show up less and less.

Failure to deliver on work from a client because of a storm and bad weather condition is out of your control. But failing to deliver because you did not prioritize, that is on you. So, know what your limits are and embrace them or strive to improve and change them.

EMBRACE IT: Accept that failure is only temporary.

Failure is not permanent nor is it fatal, you need to accept that. And if you can accept this, the experience of failure will not be overwhelming.

When you know a situation is temporary, it is easy to learn, change and adapt. Whatever the failure might be, it is a glitch in the bigger scheme of the things. Failure provides an opportunity to succeed, embrace it – it is only temporary.

How to benefit from Failure

If you ever want to succeed as much as you want to breathe, you must not only learn how to process and embrace failure but also build on the benefits that come with your experiences.

The fear of failure is possibly worse than failure itself. And one of the benefits of processing and embracing your failure is being able to face your fears. And facing your fears will make you aware of your abilities and limitations which builds character.

Facing your fear of failure empowers you to take on the next challenge which becomes a step in progress towards achieving your goals and dreams.

As you come face to face with your moments of failure you will assess, learn and adjust your progress. In the process, you will discover that failure is not permanent and therefore has no hold on you.

[
STEP INTO YOUR GREATNESS.
]

And if the lack of success is temporary, you are well equipped to forge ahead with the process, with a renewed focus and energy to start your impossible.

Winston Churchill once said, "Success is going from failure to failure without loss of enthusiasm." In essence, what he meant was, when you have had moments where you did not succeed as much as you had expected, 'without loss of enthusiasm', dust yourself off and get back in the game.

The key is to build on the lessons learned and forge ahead – fail forward. According to J.K Rowling, in a speech she gave at a University Graduation ceremony, these are the benefits of failure:

CLARITY: In crises, we find clarity. Failure forces us to clear out the noise and zone in on what really matters. Failure brings you back on track and forces you to reassess your priorities, allowing you to focus on what is truly important.

CHARACTER: If you are slammed by a setback and you are able to bounce back, it's called resilience. When you have experienced failure, your character comes into realignment with your purpose.

Crisis builds character. And a strong character is needed for the challenges that lie ahead. Character teaches you to adjust and adapt; and your bounce back is better than before.

CREATIVITY: Failure has a way of creating scarcity and constraints. To succeed, you must level up your creativity to generate fresh possibilities. I have always found that my creative juices flow in abundance when I have experienced failure.

Use this creative abundance to attract new resources to implement a renewed focus and vision.

FREEDOM: Failure brings freedom, the freedom to succeed on your own terms. Before you succeed, a part of you needs to change.

The metamorphosis of a butterfly is the best image of this change because failure strips you of the notion of invincibility. You let go of preconceived ideas of what would have, could have or should have.

Accepting failure takes an act of humility. When you take ownership of your lack of success and take the necessary steps to learn, grow and adapt – you are liberated. When you own your moment of failure, you can now go about your business without the constant pressure of faking the appearance that all is well – you are not perfect. Accepting your imperfection gives you freedom.

Realign Your Focus

From failure to failure without losing your enthusiasm – that is success. In the mind of a success champion you see your world not only as it is but also as it should be.

I have always loved the idea that all we are is a manifestation of our thoughts. Some have called it the law of attraction, yet others have referred to it as 'the secret' - whatever you call it, be prepared to use it because it has amazing power.

I remember being at a business seminar in Johannesburg – South Africa, with Robin Banks as the master of ceremony. Those who have been to any of his events will know, he has fantastic energy.

I found myself connecting to his story when he said all he has become, is the result of his thoughts and words through affirmations. On that day, I wrote down on a piece of paper what I wanted. It is an affirmation that realigns me each time I have met with a setback or huddle. It reminds me of the journey ahead.

Likewise, your thoughts expressed in words and repeated over and over again - they manifest into form. What may not seem like it, will be, because you have called upon the laws of attraction. For me, these words always remind me of where I am going, where I want to be and how I want to get there.

In reaffirming my desire to succeed, allow me to share with you the reasoning behind these words.

An affirmation, after all is a conversation with your inner being. It reaches into your soul to remind you of the things you are capable of. Very often I reaffirm my desire for success with these words, you too can do the same:

I am blessed with financial success and prosperity.

A blessing is something that is bestowed upon you without your request. Some people have called it un-requited favor. Accepting your blessing for financial success and prosperity is the first step towards success - you deserve to be successful.

Anything I set my mind to, I do.

Like starting a fire with a magnifying glass and paper, if you do not focus on one spot on the paper, the fire will not start. Set your mind on the things you want. Do not be distracted.

You need to focus all your energy and resources on the one thing at a time if you want it to work.

It takes one deal and one opportunity to turn any failure into success. Use your opportunities well. With these words profess to do whatever you set your mind to.

I find it easy to make money, because,

I am sure, like many people, you grew up in an environment that taught you making money was hard or that money does not grow on trees. These words reverse that notion of working 'hard' for money.

Remember, your financial success is a blessing, unrequited favor. Favor comes easy with an aligned focus of vision, desire, dreams and goals.

For a lot of people, one of the hardest problems to deal with is their relationship with money. If you think you need to 'Labor' for your money, chances are you will find yourself struggling to attract financial success.

I am Happy, I am Wealthy, and I am Prosperous.

They say money doesn't make you happy. Which may be true for some people, but I like to think that happy people find it easy to achieve success and prosperity – financial or otherwise. Happy people make more money.

Happy people live a life of abundance. Happy people are prosperous. That's why they find it easy to make money. Their happiness is not dependent on money, wealth and prosperity. They have all these things because choose to be happy.

When you are happy with who you are and what you want, you get to do the things you love and enjoy. Making money becomes so much easier with happiness and joy.

And I am successful beyond measure.

At his inaugural speech, Nelson Mandela quoted Marianne Williamson's poem, "Our deepest fear is not that we are inadequate. Our deepest fear is that we are powerful beyond measure."

If you are going to be successful with starting the impossible, you will need the unshakable faith and belief that 'You are successful beyond measure.'

Success is rooted in your mind. It is fixated in your creative source. And that creative source is the power of what you attract in your life.

3

FOCUS, AND KEEP YOUR EYE ON THE BALL

Most people would be more successful if they just mastered the art of focus. Yet again, failure has a way of making you lose focus. Sometimes failure is caused by the lack of focus.

The three times that I have failed, losing focus has played a big part - I took my eye off the ball. I lost focus on the vision because I was chasing the next shiny object. And the next shiny object has the way of distracting you from your vision, dreams and aspirations.

They say, 'When opportunity knocks, you must open the door.' But they don't tell you, not every opportunity is welcome into your house.

When I started in business, I wanted to go into marketing and adverting, more in the line of media communications.

> # I ALREADY KNOW
> # WHAT IT'S LIKE TO
> # GIVE UP

A friend of mine invited me to a presentation for network marketing and I was excited at the thought of making money through other people's effort.

Without thought or understanding if this opportunity was aligned to my vision, I signed up. To my disappointment, I never really made it in that business. This is not to say network marketing does not work, but my understanding of it, limited my success.

Years later, I was running a Marketing and Promotions company, doing below the line marketing – in-store promotions, activations and events.

Again, a friend of mine invited me to collaborate in a design and marketing agency. That too went bust, not entirely because of the lack of focus but that did play a part in us not achieving the goals we set out to achieve.

My last experience, when I established RedOystor Media – our focus was publishing and publications, yet again a good mentor of mine, a person I highly respected invited me to partner in the business of educating people about investing in the stock market and training them on how to start an online business.

That too didn't work out. You might want to guess the reason we did not succeed – among other things, loss of focus. We lost focus on the task at hand.

Some things look a lot alike, but they are not the same. Your goal may be similar to someone else's, but the journey is not the same - pick your focus.

Don't get me wrong, there are many other factors that led to a lack of success in many of these businesses – not the right fit for partnerships, misalignment of vision but FOCUS had a lot to do on my part.

When you lose focus of the vision, you lose focus of the goals you want to achieve.

In reality, while many opportunities are attractive and may possibly make for a great return on your investment, remember this; 'Not every opportunity that knocks at your door deserves to be let into the house.' The greatest lesson you may soon have to learn is how to say 'NO' to the things that are not aligned with your dreams.

Get Back into Alignment

I hear a lot of would be entrepreneurs or aspiring business people say things like, "I'm hustling."

Sad part, we all seem to be doing the same thing 'Hustling'. I think it's time we stopped the 'hustle'. In a fast-paced world, where you are constantly bombarded with information from left, right and center, it can be hard to focus on what is really important which leads to this 'Hustling' phenomenon.

Most people wake up in the morning thinking about the next challenge, the next project, how to get to work, how to make sure the kids are taken care off – basically the 'hustle' and bustle of life. In all of that they lose focus on the one thing they should be working on.

It Starts with a Vision

One of my sons was asked in pre-primary what he wanted to be when he grows up. I am told, his response was, 'I want to be my Daddy.'

The little guy had no cooking clue what I did for a living, but he wanted to be me. When asked 'Why?' I was told he said, 'Because my Daddy makes people happy with jobs, and free things.'

That last part, I guess he saw the promotional items being given away for free and that made people happy. Sadly, I don't remember what I wanted to be when I was growing up. One thing I know, the freedom to do whatever I wanted to do was top of my list.

I remember playing with paper money and telling my friends I would be a 'Zillionaire'. Since 'Z' was the last letter of the alphabet, I figured I wanted to be rich on the last level.

I didn't know what it meant to be rich but I surely had an idea that Rich People have the freedom to be, whoever and whatever they want to be - and I wanted the freedom to choose, the ability to live without lacking the most basic of life's necessities. I have since learned it is possible to achieve this kind of lifestyle as an entrepreneur.

I don't know what you wanted to be when you grew up, however I am hoping with this book, you will be able to tap into that childhood memory to find out what sets your heart on fire.

Likewise, over the years my vision has been refined – I want to be a person of influence, to touch lives and see the world as better place.

It's crazy to think that I can change the world, but then again, Steve Jobs said:

Here's to the crazy ones, the misfits, the trouble makers, the round pegs in square holes…the ones who see things different.

They are not fond of rules, you can quote them, disagree with them, glorify or vilify them, but the only thing you can't do is ignore them because they change things.

They push the human race forward, and while many may see them as the crazy ones, we see genius, because the ones who are crazy enough to think they can change the world, are the ones who do.

Allow me to add, "…the ones who are crazy enough to think they can start the impossible, are the ones who usually do."

It starts with a vision. What's yours?

It may not be clear at the beginning but as you traverse the great lengths of your boundaries, pushing beyond your comfort zone, reach for the impossible. Great experiences are made of dreams.

It is not crazy to want to live the life of your dreams, so you must dream as much as you want and as much as you can. If you are crazy enough to think you can change the world, trust me, you can do just that.

For as long as your vision is clear, your goals and goal posts on the journey of life will guide you if you maintain focus on what you want to achieve. When you experience failure, your vision will bring you back into focus. Hence the reason you may have to fail before you can succeed - it is one of the benefits of failure; bringing you back into focus.

When you experience failure, vision will take you away from the 'hustle' of life to an alignment of purpose. When you experience failure, vision will redirect you to your point of prosperity. A place where you do not have to 'Hustle' to achieve the things you want to achieve.

When your vision is in alignment with your desires, dreams and aspirations, it is easy to reaffirm "I am blessed with financial success and prosperity" because you know that you deserve the blessings. When your vision is intact, you make it possible to affirm "Anything I set my mind to, I do." When your vision is clear, you can profess, "I am successful beyond measure."

The Power of Focus

In the first episode of Star Wars, Qui-Gon shares some great Jedi wisdom with Anakin, "Always remember, your focus determines your reality."

Here's a truth I will share with you at no extra cost, if you wake up in the morning thinking about the miserable things that happened the night before, chances are you will have a miserable day. What you focus on amplifies, since you are going to be focusing anyway, why not focus on success.

Remember Don Shula's 24-hour philosophy on celebrating your victories or licking your wounds, each morning should start with a readiness to take on the next challenge. If you focus is on failure, it will become a regular reality. But if your focus is on success, that too will become your regular reality.

Focus on the Now

Anxiety is created by the anticipation of a future we cannot predict but focusing on the present can do a lot to help you succeed when you have failed.

Apart from being able to increase your effectiveness, focusing on the now reduces stress and helps you enjoy the journey towards starting the impossible.

The past is gone, let it go. The only useful thing about yesterday is the lessons you should learn. The best part about today, is that you have the opportunity to change what you want to see and be in your tomorrow.

Think of the things you can be doing right now that will change your tomorrow. If you must start a business, think about your business model, the product or service and clients or customers you want to serve. Think about the value you want to give in exchange for a reward for your efforts.

How will you execute your plans and what must you do now that will get your plan rolling? Think in terms of the now. What must happen now to make tomorrow better. If it means registering your business with the state authorities, do it now - get the process started. If it means you need to go to the bank to open an account, don't wait until someone needs to pay you, do it now - your actions don't have to wait until tomorrow.

If it means you need to make a sales call to your potential clients, send that proposal to your investors, or submit your resume to a prospective employer, there is no better time than the present.

I have one simple motto, 'Do one thing every day that gets you closer to your vision, dreams and aspirations.' With a focus on that 'one thing', it starts to add up. As the Chinese proverb says 'The journey of a thousand miles begins with a single step. Focus on that one thing every day and you will achieve the impossible.

Focus on the Goals

Success is made up of a series of achievements – these are your goals. In my experience, focusing on your goals can yield many positive results.

If you maintain your focus on your goals, surely you will achieve success. I'm sure you have heard of SMART goals. If not, may I suggest that you Google and read a little more about them, they will change your life.

On one of our online publication you will also find a simplified version of what smart goals are. Use the following link for direct access www.thinkwealthmaga-zine.com/definition-of-smart-goals

Understanding SMART goals will enable you to plan your life with ease, both personal and profession. All with the kind of skill to help you better achieve your dreams.

Keep your goals 'Specific' – Say 'I want to start a business selling apparel clothing on the Internet.' Or 'I want to earn an income working as an accountant.' The simpler, the better. Specify what you what to do and how you plan to achieve it.

$$\left[\ \ \text{...I WANT TO SEE WHAT HAPPENS IF I DON'T.}\ \ \right]$$

Be specific about what you want. It cannot be vague, it needs to be clear in your mind what you want and how you want it.

I want to be a millionaire is vague, but I want to earn $100,000 every month for the next ten years is specific. Get your goal to be specific.

Ask yourself, 'What do I want?' 'How will I get it?'; 'With whom will I have to work with to get it?' And all other specifics. These things need to be clear or at least have a sense of clarity.

Your goals should be 'Measurable' – You need to identify what the successful achievement of your goals looks and feels like.

You want to have an idea of what the road looks like before you get to the destination, but also what the destination looks like, so you know how to identify with it. You don't have to have been there to know what it looks like, but you have to have an idea.

By when do you want to start your clothing business? By when do you want to have your business operating and selling?

How will you know it is working or not working? How many sales do you need to be making in order to remain in business and become profitable?

What you cannot measure, you cannot monitor. You want to be able to monitor your goals. The only way to know if you are succeeding is to monitor how far you have come from where you started.

The physical manifestation of your goals should be clear in your mind's eye.

Make your goals 'Attainable' - However keep this in mind, if the target is too big, whichever way you shoot, you will hit. Unless your aim is really bad.

Dream big, remembering that big is relative; my big and your big are different. To an ant, an apple is big. To an apple, a human is big. To the human, an elephant is big.

I don't need to go on, you get the picture. Big is relative and so decide what is 'Your Big' idea. Is it a corner shop at the mall or is a franchise throughout the country?

Whatever your big is, make it attainable. It is pointless to target a million-dollar deal when you have not attained a thousand dollar deal. Take small steps, strive for big achievements – so dream big, however be prepared to start small.

Each victory builds confidence for the next challenge. If you have no time, money, talent and resources to achieve your goals, you need to reach into your creative source to make that possible and attainable.

Your goals need to be 'Relevant' - Not only to you but also to your vision. I have seen people fail because they were in competition with an irrelevant person. The question you want to ask, 'Are the goals you have set relevant to you?'

$$\left[\; \textbf{DON'T STOP IF YOU HAVEN'T TRIED TO FAIL.} \;\right]$$

Remember 'big' is relative. If your big idea is to have the most successful clothing store in a particular city or state, is it relevant to set a goal of running a multinational organization.

Your goals should be relevant to your measurable and attainable specifics. Whatever is irrelevant will not drive you.

Start with the 'Why?' Why do you want to reach that goal? Why is this goal relevant to the vision you have for your life? How will achieving this goal change your life? Basically, you want to know if the goals you set are relevant to you.

Put 'Time' into your goals – They say time is money, and you cannot waste either. Without a deadline for when you want to achieve your goals, you only have a wish. Put a deadline to your goals – 'I want to earn

$100,000 per month over the next ten years starting from the 1st of January 2020'.

Putting unrealistic timing to your goals will only hurt your success. While the objective is not to set a race against time, what you need is goal posts as indicators to help guide your progress – putting time-lines to your goals does that for you. Maintaining focus on your goals will help you achieve the impossible.

Through my failed experiences, I lost focus on the vision and therefore my goals were misaligned. When I wanted to be in Marketing and Communications, network marketing was not my area of focus. Later when I was in promotions and activations, design was not my area of focus. These may have been interrelated, but they were not the area of focus.

Keeping your goals in focus means saying 'No' to other things that are not in alignment with your dream.

For your own sanity, learning to say 'NO' to what is not a priority to your success is a skill you will soon have to learn. Give time to the areas where you are the most productive. Set targets on when you want to attain your desired outcomes.

Focus on the Positive

The mind is a powerful weapon. It will take you to places you can only imagine. To start the impossible, the companionship of a positive mind opens you up to a great experience.

With a positive mind, you know you have the backing of a thoroughly capable power source. To achieve success, your focus on the positive will help you navigate through challenges and obstacles at a faster pace than if you entertain negative thoughts.

The human mind is exposed to over 50 thousand thoughts on any given day – mental chatter, images and blockbuster movies playing out in our heads. Over 90% of these thoughts are a repetition of past experiences, which 80% is habitual negative thinking.

Success needs you to learn how to focus your thinking not on the negative but the positive. More so, you want to focus on what you want and not what you do not what.

Avoid saying things like, 'I don't want to fail'. Instead say 'I want to succeed.' Do not say 'I cannot afford it.' Rather say 'How can I afford it. Can you imagine Howard Hill, one of the greatest archers of all time - he is known to have won 196 Archery Tournaments in succession?

If you gave Howard Hill his best bow and arrow, blind folded him and span him a couple of times, then tell him to shoot on a target. I bet my life savings, he would miss the target. Why? Because with his eyes closed and his focus not on the target he is bound to miss.

The same applies to you. You will miss every opportunity that is out of your area of focus.

Let your target be the positive. Aim for what you want instead of worrying about what you don't want. What we think, we feel, and therefore our thinking has a direct impact on our emotions and outcomes.

What we feel we act on.

It is these actions that are directed by our focus which in many ways influences what we attract into our lives.

One of the greatest skills I have learned is how to be aware of my negative thoughts. Over time I have mastered how to replace those negative thoughts with positive ones.

In business and many other areas in your life, there will be times when you feel like giving up, if you entertain these negative thoughts, they grow and fester into negative emotions which lead to negative actions and wanting to give up.

> # TRY AND FAIL... AND TRY AGAIN UNTIL YOU SUCCEED.

To achieve the impossible, teach your mind to focus on positive thoughts. Think about how great you feel about the next challenge.

Think about how great it would be to finally achieve your dreams. Think about how happy you would be when you conquered your fears and overcome setbacks to be where you want to be. Focus on the positive.

Focus on the task at hand

Too many times when we are trying to get back on our feet after a massive fall, private or public failure, we tend to fall for any opportunity that promises the possibility of a positive outcome.

I don't know how many people have lost money chasing money. As a result, we fall for get-rich-quick schemes that take us for a ride. There is no such thing as a quick buck. Money is attracted to you, don't chase it, call it. Money comes because you have earned it or worked for it.

You don't have to work 'Hard' in the traditional sense of the word, but you must apply yourself to realizing the financial reward. Applying yourself entails focusing on the task at hand.

I have found that focusing on the task at hand yields better results that trying to have your hand in every pot. As the Chinese would say, 'He that chases two rabbits catches neither.'

Have you ever lost yourself in an activity you were so passionate about that you forgot what was happing around you? If you are to start your impossible, finding this passion is important in many ways.

People find great enjoyment not in mindless activity but in actions that bring fulfillment to their soul. I am like that. If whatever I am doing isn't fulfilling, I find it hard to follow through.

The question would be, how do you get into the flow of focusing on the task at hand. Remember, starting your impossible is about getting up, dusting yourself and shooting for the stars.

Well here's a basic way to get you started.

Find something you are passionate about. I always say, to succeed, you need to lose yourself in the service of others. And this is an extremely important step at kick starting your success. Find a hobby you are passionate about and just immerse yourself in it. Find a cause you are passionate about, volunteer and get involved.

Go into the great outdoors and just do something that truly engages you. While you're at it, shut off all distractions and let your mind be occupied by the one thing that sets your heart on fire.

What has worked for me is going off the grid – no TV, no Social Media and no unnecessary distractions. I do a lot more gym, running, sports, hobbies, writing and a lot of time with family and very close friends. All the things that bring me back into focus on what I want to achieve and why I want to achieve it.

When I have found that passion, I get back to the task at hand. It is this passion that brings you back into focus. Begin by working each task diligently to completion.

The milestones you make with each successful task, you ignite the flame you need to keep going. Achieving small victories yields giant steps.

Brain Tracy in his book 'Eat that Frog' talks about starting with the hardest task and working your way to the easiest - do that. It makes completing the task at hand so much easier. When the hardest task is done, the rest will only be a breeze to complete.

I have a simple process that ensures I get a lot done on any given day. I call it the 'five steps' process to achieving the impossible. The starting point is the 80/20 rule, which says – 20% of what you do will give you 80% of the result and 80% of your actions will only result is 20% of your achievements.

STEP 1: Based on your goals, write down 5 to 10 tasks you wanted completed that will get you achieving your goals and dreams. The best time to plan these tasks is the night before; just before going to bed. Let them percolate and seamer into your subconscious while you sleep. It helps to think about them the night before because your brain can work on them through the night.

STEP 2: Order your 5 or 10 tasks by priority – the most important, the hardest to complete and the ones that require your greatest attention at the top of your list. You will want to focus your mind on the most important task or tasks.

STEP 3: Focus on the 20% and carry them through to completion. If you have 5 tasks, you have one task that needs your undivided attention. If it is 10 tasks, then you will have two that need you focus.

Start each task as early as when you wake up – the earlier the better. I like to work at 4 am in the morning after a morning jog, while my mind is still fresh and when there are very few distractions.

STEP 4: Once you have completed your priority tasks, start working on your other tasks as and when your time is available.

Wherever possible, delegate whatever is no longer a priority. While you can do most things on your own, getting help will get you achieving the impossible much faster.

STEP 5: Review and renew. This is when you go through your day's activities as they relate to achieving your goals, dreams and aspirations. What you have done and completed, was it a success or failure.

If it was a failure, how would you do it differently next time – find the lessons and learn from them. Any tasks you delegate - follow up and follow through on them, you are still accountable for their completion.

Repeat these steps each day, with each task until you start to see a positive result in your actions.

If you continue to experience failure, call in the reinforcements – coaches, advisor and trusted confidants. Better yet, read this book again. You may have missed one or two steps to the processes of achieving the impossible.

Focus on your Commitment

It is said, there are three types of people in the word. Those that make things happened, those that watch things happen and those that wonder what happened.

Of these three only the people who make things happen get to enjoy the fruit of their success. Why? Because they were committed to the process of getting things done.

Starting the impossible requires that you block all other distractions and just focus your commitment to achieving your goals, dreams and aspirations. Distractions will be there. Daily you will find yourself inundated with activities that need your attention. Select with is priority, and delegate what is not.

Commit to the process of getting things done.

You may have made some errors in the past. You may have taken some decisions that had negative outcomes, but your focused commitment to achieving the impossible is what sets you apart from other unsuccessful people.

To start, honor commitments to yourself before you make commitments to others. Make a commitment to yourself that each day you will do one thing that will lead to achieving your vision. Commit to showing up for yourself every single time and that commitment will carry over to showing up for others.

Without a focus on your own commitment to achieve your vision, you cannot expect to do that for the people around you. It's often said, charity begins at home. Start by making a commitment to planning your goals, acting on your plans and learning from whatever experiences life throws at you.

Reaffirm your Focus

People who focus on what they want tend to prosper. Those that don't struggle. Failure is a lack of success when you are not focused on what you want. When your vision is not clear, the distractions of life take away your focus from what you desire and deserve – which is success.

You will be tempted to chase the next opportunity because it knocked on your door screaming 'Trick or Treat'. But never sacrifice what you truly want for what you want right now.

Don't settle for less than you deserve. Be patient, great things take time.

To clear my mind and reaffirm my focus on the vision ahead of me, I go jogging as early as 4am every other day. As I run, I repeat the words that have become my affirmation.

With every word, the picture becomes clearer and clearer. I know now what I want, and I hope with these words, you too are finding clarity in your vision. Let them sink in. Let them ignite your spark.

Let your focus fuel your desire to succeed. Reaffirmed your focus with these words:

I am blessed with financial success and prosperity.

Anything I set my mind to, I do.

I find it easy to make money, because,

I am Happy, I am Wealthy, and I am Prosperous.

Most recently I have made additions to my affirmation as part of my SMART goals and the impact I want to have on the world.

Inspired by Zig Ziglar who said, 'If you help enough people get what they want, you will get what you want.'

It doesn't matter what you do, if you are a teacher and you teach well and give students what they want 'Which is knowledge and good grades', you will get what you want.

You might ask, Vukani, what do you want?

Well, I want to be an Entrepreneur - a problem solver, a solutions finder and above all that, I want to be happy - to make friends and influence people.

And so I add:

I make at least a million dollars a month for myself and for my business.

These words speak to my personal and business goals over the next 5 to 10 years.

I'm a creator of a thousand millionaires

It's not about the money, it's about the value and impact of your influence. The money is the measure by which you aim to achieve your goal.

And I am successful beyond measure.

There is no time like the present and it needs you to focus. When you have failed, to start the impossible, you need to bounce back – better than you were before.

4 BOUNCE BACK

L et's be real, we've all messed up in our lives at one point or another. What matters is how you handled your mess and the message that comes with it – will you get better or will you get worse.

Failure is failure. Big or small, private or public, failure is all the same. You may have failed an exam. Or failed in business, marriage or any other area of your life, how you bounce back determines how well you can aim and shoot for the stars. Whatever your aim is, if you keep your eye on the ball, eventually you will hit your target.

Let's say you've analyzed your mess. You've admitted to your mistakes and you have owned up to the reality that you and you alone can make a change – to start your impossible – you need to bounce back. And bounce back fast.

Like the law of attraction, which operates on basic principles - what you think you feel, and what you feel you act out or act on. Often shortened to 'What you think you become.'

Bouncing back to start your impossible has simple Principles that form the foundation of your success.

PRINCIPLE 1: Find Stability

When you are falling, unless you have stable ground on which to stand on, you'll be grasping on branches. Grasping at straws? Half the time you are grasping on things that have little value.

What you must understand is, unless whatever you're grasping on has a solid grip, you have no chance of success. It's easy to hold on to the past. It's understandable that you would want to feel connected to a part of you that's familiar. However painful it might be, it is the devil you know. What we don't realize is, holding on can hurt your chance of success - so you need to learn to let go.

Letting go is possibly the hardest thing to do for any one that is falling and failing. Often, we don't know if it is a test of our resilience or an opportunity for course correction. And because of that, we are never too sure when to hold on or let go.

Finding stability is easy. It requires that you let go of anything that no longer serves your vision. Anything that no longer supports your goals has no room in your life. It becomes an Achilles heel, holding you back on the most important journey in your life - personal discovery.

I remember a picture of a man who was holding on for dear life on a branch off a cliff. The people above kept screaming "Let go, you will be fine." But he wouldn't or at least he thought he couldn't. When he finally did let go, he discovered he was less than one foot away from stable ground.

Often, we hold on because we think letting go is a sign of failure. Not realizing, if we don't let go, we may not discover the many other opportunities that life seeks to present us with.

Stability in your Environment

Finding stability may mean you'll need to let go of certain people in your life, habits and practices you may have grown accustom to or projects and activities that no longer server the greater vision of where you want to be.

It's been suggested that you are the average of the five people closest to you. The people you spend your most time with. Over time you adopt and adapt many of their traits, characters and characteristics.

In order to create a stable environment for your growth, you may need a change of environment. Not just the area you stay in but also the people you surround yourself with. With regards to the people around you, here is a criterion by which to make your selection. This is a guide, not cast in stone, but will help you find the right association with the people who may exert influence in your life:

1. **They must be inspired.** Inspiration in an outward expression of an internal desire. If the people around you don't have that burning fire, soon yours will start to die off as well.

2. **They must be passionate.** Passion is desire expressed in actions. Surround yourself with people that are obsessed with taking action, and you will achieve the impossible.

3. **They must be motivated.** Motivation is like taking a bath, it may not be essential for most people but highly recommended if you want to avoid what Zig Ziglar termed 'stinking thinking'. You will need to stay motivated by being around people that are just as motivated.

4. **They must be grateful.** Gratitude is the foundation of success. If you cannot be grateful for the little that you have you can never be entrusted with more. Grateful people will appreciate your efforts and celebrate your successes.

5. **They must be open minded.** For change to happen, you need to be open to the possibility that there is a better or different way of doing things. It would have been stupid of Thomas Edison to repeat the same mistake with hopes for a different outcome. Albert Einstein would have called him insane.

Find stability in your environment by surrounding

yourself with people who share similar goals, values and principles.

Stability in your Foundation

They say the best part about hitting rock bottom is that you know the only way out is up. Rock bottom provides stability for you to plan your next move. Rock bottom allows you to prepare yourself for the next challenge with stable grounding.

I remember the first time I hit rock bottom, I had a 6-month-old baby, a wife who was looking to me to provide for the family and family that had great expectations on my achievements. I had to find stability.

My stability involved having a roof over my head, that coupled with an income to support my family, my health and myself. The base from which you launch your impossible needs to be stable.

I had the privilege of family support. People I could count on to help me bounce back and recover while I worked on taking on the impossible. When the time came, I relaunched my career as an Entrepreneur with a solid foundation.

PRINCIPLE 2: Earn an Income

Jobs are overrated, at least that is what I think. Income is what you need. Getting that income may mean you get a job, but it's not A JOB you should focus on as your source of income.

After my first 'mess up' in business back in 2008, I

remember thinking to myself 'I need to get a JOB'. And everybody else told me 'You need to get a JOB.' After some introspection, I realized I was missing the point. What sobered me up was the reminder that the job's only purpose was to earn an income. And so, I abandoned the JOB idea in search of an income.

Together with the people who were under my roof. We started a paper and plastic recycling business which kept us going for a while. It provided the income we needed to bounce back. The work was not glamorous however, it gave us the confidence to try again. And you need income to get your started.

Income is tied to confidence, so you must work to earn an income as you bounce back. The confidence you get from being able to afford your life, take care of yourself and those around you, is valuable.

As an entrepreneur, I've worked in many companies not because I needed a job but because I needed to build courage and confidence while earning an income. I've sold everything from alarm systems to insurance and training programs.

If life was a car, income would be the fuel by which you keep things going, so you need it. You can have a car with a powerful engine, beautiful body with features from here to the future but without gas, you are going nowhere slowly. And so, need an income.

Walt Disney worked as a newspaper editor to earn an income – which he was fired from because apparently, he lacked imagination. That part of his life gave him an opportunity to earn an income.

Jack Ma worked as an English teacher and sometimes

an English translator to earn an income while he was building the Alibaba empire. Elon Musk was the janitor of a boiler room in a lumber mill. He might not talk about it, however that is the part of his life that launched the Elon Musk we know today.

Madonna was a cashier at Dunkin' Donuts and Jeff Bezos was a cashier at McDonald's. Swallow your pride, you need to earn an income if you are ever going to realize your dreams and succeed at starting the impossible.

THINK IT... DREAM IT... AND LIVE UP TO IT.

All of these successful people took up these jobs not because they needed a job, but because they needed an income to sustain them while they worked on starting and launching their careers. It was the foundation they needed at a time when everything was falling apart.

They might have not called it an income at the time when they were working the J.O.B. Whatever you call it - the main hustle while you build your side hustle. The 9-5 that allows you to build your 5-9. Either way, you are going to need an income, if you are going to succeed at building your next big idea.

The impossible is not possible if you cannot survive the day to day. Launching the impossible is difficult when you cannot feed, clothe and take care of your well-being - you need to be alive to see it through.

Personally, I've worked as a call center sales agent for

more than 2 years to earn an income. More than anything you build courage in your ability and confidence in your skills while earning an income.

PRINCIPLE 3: Build Courage and Confidence

Henri Bergson said, 'Think like a man of action; act like a man of thought.' Every action is born out of a feeling and every feeling is the result of a thought. Confidence gets you started, courage keeps you going.

To start your impossible, you need to find time to place your mind in the right frame to take MASSIVE action. That is only possible with courage and confidence.

I've already mentioned that earning an income boosts your confidence and builds courage. However, you can do more than income to get to the next level. And when the income part is sorted, you are able to work on becoming the best version of yourself for even greater success.

The Greater Good Science Centre at UC Berkeley created a very practical model to build courage and confidence in your self – they called it the Best Possible Self, and this is how you do it.

Take a moment to imagine a better future for your yourself – you have the car of your dreams, the house you've always wanted to live in, with a great career and a beautiful family that supports your vision, dreams and goals. Do this for three weeks at least twice a day.

Keep a journal, write down everything you would like to achieve. Write down the kind of person you want to become and the goals you want to achieve.

Reflect on it daily. You may also use a vision board if you are more visual. You get to see your future the way you want it.

I started doing this in the morning before I go running and at night before I go to bed – I have not stopped since. Each time I reflect on the future I want to create. While I do this exercise, I repeat my mantra and affirmation:

I am blessed with financial success and prosperity.

Anything I set my mind to, I do.

I find it easy to make money, because,

I am Happy, I am Wealthy, and I am Prosperous.

I make at least a million dollars a month for myself and for my business.

I'm a creator of a thousand millionaires

And I am successful beyond measure.

With each word I feel my confidence and courage build up so much so that I can take on anything in the world. You need that fire to drive you from within.

It is not possible to get positive results on a negative mindset. Negative thoughts have never produced positive actions. Think about what you want, not what you don't want. Think along the lines of 'I want to be happy' as opposed to 'I don't want to be sad.' Think, 'I want a rewarding career' as opposed to 'I hate this JOB.' Your thoughts affect your actions.

Be specific about where you want to be, the kind of person you want to be and the environment you want to be in. You will be amazed how being specific produces the kind of energy that yields result.

Be as creative and as imaginative as you can be and don't worry about your last failed moment, just focus on what you want and aim for that.

This exercise is most effective when coupled with practical experience on living your mantra and affirmation – step out of your comfort zone and do something that challenges you.

Go running. Do yoga or join a dancing class. Learn a new language. It's not about the activity you take.

It's about the experience of a new kind of adventure that allows you to challenge yourself and your abilities.

I find that speaking with people fuels my drive and so I make it a point to speak to as many people as possible. I walk into a restaurant; first instinct is to greet the waiters and applaud them for the great work they do. It's my way of sending out positive energy from within.

For you, it might be getting a new job. Starting a home-based business. Helping a friend out when they don't necessarily pay you - what matters is that you are using your energy to deliver a full dose of possibility.

PRINCIPLE 4: Partner with the Right People

Here is a sobering reality you're going to have to face – you cannot do it on your own. For Apple INC to succeed, Steve Jobs had Steve Wozwick.

For Microsoft Bill Gates had Paul Allen and Larry

Page had Sergey Brin at Google; you too are going to need to find a person or people to partner with to achieve the impossible. You may be able to do it on your own, but it helps to have a partner.

You'll need to partner with people with whom you have productive relationships.

The best combinations are always people who compliment your skills as opposed to people who have the same skill set as you.

It sounds noble to have friends with whom you share common interests, skills and ideals, however if you want to achieve the impossible, challenge yourself. If you are an Entrepreneur, you may need to partner with a business manager to manage the operations.

If you are an introvert, you may need the skills of an extrovert, someone who will be out going when you are not.

How you and your partner or partners complement each other forms the foundation of a productive relationship.

Whatever partnership you build on, you will need people who recognize your limitations as well as theirs but also respect what you and they bring to the table. It should always be a mutually beneficial relationship.

If you ever find yourself in a relationship where you are putting in more than the other person, walk out.

It will not serve your vision, goals and desire for success. If you ever find yourself in a relationship where your partner or partners are taking more than they give, walk out, it will cripple your success.

As Robert Kiyosaki said in his book Rich Dad, Poor Dad - an asset puts money in your pocket; a liability takes money out of your pocket. Treat your relationships with your partner or partners in the same way.

Partner with assets and you will grow and be rewarded, and you should also be an asset to the relationship.

Be the kind of partner that brings value.

PRINCIPLE 5: Step up and Take action

Your dreams, vision, aspirations and desires are only as good as the actions you take to achieve them. Everything you do as you bounce back should be a build up to taking MASSIVE action.

When you dream, wake up and take action. Whatever you desire, get up and take action. When you wish upon a star, open your eyes and take action.

Nothing happens unless you take action.

Every step of the way, whatever you do, remember without taking action, your vision, dreams and goals are nothing more than wishes without the prospect of ever coming to life.

There is no other way that I can tell you to take action except to remind you of something that is very profound about the film and movie industry.

Can you imagine if the director on any set would scream the words – 'Lights, Camera...' But never 'Action.' Nothing will come to life. We would have no movies to watch and no stories to tell. All because the director neglected to scream 'Action'.

You are the director in your life. You are also the actor and the executive producer. Every day is a piece of script building up to the blockbuster you were born to be.

If you are going to live the best life, as you have dreamed, you're going to have to step up and take action.

You may dream all you want. You may think all you want. You may even plan all you want but if you never take action nothing will come to life.

In your vision your lights will come on. As you plan, focus your camera on the things that matter most. Everything else is just a distraction. But more importantly, take action.

Not just any action, take MASSIVE action. And you will be greatly rewarded.

Taking action means, making that sales call to introduce your company. Following up on the email to the job applications you sent through.

Taking action means finishing the proposal you started writing and sending it to the relevant person. Every part of the process leads to the manifestation of your goals.

Taking action may also mean submitting that resignation letter because you are ready to start the impossible. And with these words I aim to fuel your imagination to see the opportunity ahead of you. Repeat after me:

I am blessed with financial success and prosperity.

Anything I set my mind to, I do.

I find it easy to make money, because,

I am Happy, I am Wealthy, and I am Prosperous.

I make at least a million dollars a month for myself and for my business.

I'm a creator of a thousand millionaires

And I am successful beyond measure.

You want to believe you have the power to achieve the impossible – and you must.

You want to accept that even though you may have failed not once or twice but many times – you have the spirit of resilience that charges at the impossible.

It is time you know that against all odds, setbacks and failures. Your 'mess' is a message to the new you – and you will be impossible to stop when you reach out and shoot for the stars.

5

START YOUR IMPOSSIBLE

Lisa Amos once said, "Entrepreneurs average 3.8 failures before their final success." Personally, I've had 3 major fails so far and so I'm short 0.8. The success of this book will either prove her right or challenge me for another try.

She goes on to say, "What sets the successful ones apart is their amazing persistence." Their ability to move from failure to failure without losing enthusiasm. You may not be an entrepreneur, but I am sure you have seen your fair share of fails. And if you are, you can re-late.

The main reason you're going to succeed at starting your impossible is not because you read this book. Granted, it will restart your desire for success, which will lead to you taking massive action to see through the impossible and finally taking on the challenge to keep pushing until you have a break through.

I read a quote that said, "The river does not break through rocks and mountains because of its strength; it does so because of its persistence."

You are a river flowing - full of life. In front of you stands giant mountains of impossibility. With a nudge in the right direction, a change of mind set and your 'amazing persistence' you will succeed.

It was at 4am on a cold winter's day. I had just submitted my resignation from the company I was working for at that time. I had done my time. I had recovered and bounced back and ready to start my impossible.

The air around me was fresh. As it penetrated my lungs, I found myself flamed by the possibility of a beautiful life. A life I had dreamed of for many years. I had planned my impossible. I had visions of what it would be like to step out and step up. I was flanked by the confidence and courage I had gained from being around amazing people where I worked.

With one foot in front of another, my jogging pace increased my heart rate. I fell in love with the tomorrow I had in my mind.

At face value I had nothing, but in the depth of my soul I had the vision of a titan and the spirit of a worrier. As I was running these words came back to me like a flood on a mission:

*I am blessed with financial success and
prosperity.*

Anything I set my mind to, I do.

I find it easy to make money, because,

*I am Happy, I am Wealthy, and I am
Prosperous.*

Repeated over and over again I said them louder and
louder. But how would I know and measure what success looks and feels like to me. Remember, your goals
have to be SMART and in rhythmic thought these words
came to life:

*I make at least a million dollars a month for
myself and for my business.*

I'm a creator of a thousand millionaires.

When I said these words, I had an epiphany. It's more
than just the financial reward. It's about the people you
touch, the influence you have to set a different agenda of
the world we want to live in.

A place where my child and your child have the opportunity to dream as their fathers and mothers had an
opportunity to dream, because:

I am successful beyond measure.

If you have never been on the road to find yourself,
try it, you will soon discover the impossible is possibility
disguised as hard work and persistence.

Zig Ziglar called it priming the pump. I call it starting your impossible. You may have been told what is and what is not possible. For a child, standing up is impossible because their bones are not strong enough to hold their weight.

For a child, getting onto the bed is impossible because they can barely reach for the seam of the bed. Many things look and feel impossible because you're progress in the process of success.

It's impossible for a janitor at a boiler maker to become the most successful innovator of all time – but Elon Musk saw through the impossible. Is it impossible for a vacuum cleaner salesman to take on the world of blockbuster movies – Reed Hasting saw through the impossibility with Netflix.

It is impossible for a McDonald's cashier to imagine themselves as the most successful ecommerce giant in the history of business – Jeff Bezos saw through the impossible to succeed at Amazon. It doesn't matter what your current circumstances are, what's your impossible. Define it, plan it, qualify it, then step up and take MASSIVE action.

ONE: Define your impossible

What is your big idea? What is your big vision? What is it that you really want? What does success look like to you?

What will it feel like when you have achieved the impossible? Will that make you smile with content or challenge you with an even bigger dream.

Define your impossible. Is it the smell of a new luxury German car? Is it the keys to your new home?

Is it the signature on the million-dollar deal or is it the banking notification of a hundred million dollars transferred into your account?

You need to imagine it to define it. It needs to be very clear in your mind's eye what you want. You need to define it to identify with it when you do finally achieve it. How else will you know what success looks if you cannot clearly define its shape, form and feel.

[

FOR OTHERS TO BELIEVE IN YOU...

]

Your impossible cannot be vague. It needs to be real. Get yourself a journal or a notebook and write down what you want but deem to be impossible. Meditate and think about it on a daily basis. Your mind will be occupied with the need to find a solution to your impossible.

Think of your impossible as possible. Write down how you want to achieve your impossible. Your plans may not work as well as you have written them down, however your mind will start to seek the solutions it needs to achieve the goals you have set out.

TWO: Plan your impossible

It's time to get back on the horse and create the next phase of your life. The past is gone, and your future awaits. Those that fail to plan simply plan to fail. Success is not an accident.

Ask yourself, "What can I possibly do to get back to the top?"

"Who do I need to bring into my circle of confidence to help me get back on the mount?"

"What actions do you need to take to achieve your goals and dreams?"

How many calls do you need to make a day to close a sale? If in business, practically plan your business. How many prospective employers do you need to contact for an interview? How will you earn your income while you work on your big dream? All of these need a plan.

As I said before, get a journal, write it down. Review it at least once a week for your short-term goals and once a month for your long term challenges.

I have a simple 3-step process that has worked for me over the past couple of years. Below I share it with you because I believe and I'm confident it would work for you as well.

STEP 1: Write your goals in the positive present tense. As you will see in my mantra, everything 'I am' not 'I will'. Think about what you want to become, and write it down as being just that.

If you want to be a doctor, write that you are a doctor. Write that you are a successful doctor. You may only be a student or a student doctor, or a doctor in the making. In your plan, you are a doctor. The same applies for any other goals you set.

After you have decided on who and what you are,

write your goals as resolutions on actions you want to take to achieve those goals. This is where 'I will' comes into play. 'I will start jogging every day at 4am in the morning for 30 minutes' will get you better results than 'I want to lose weight.'

STEP 2: Share your goals with your circle of confidence - your partner or partners, close confident or a coach and advisor. Sharing your goals with your circle of influence gives you the benefit of instant support from people who have a vested interest in your success. Often you will find this leads to a conversation of how they can support you.

Be prepared to listen and learn but remember this is your plan. If you are going to succeed at achieving your impossible, you have to put it into action. If you don't believe in the choices you make, you will never hold yourself accountable to the actions you take.

STEP3: Do one thing every day that gets you closer to your dream. When you dream is big, it can be scary and exciting all at the same time. Each day take one action, one step to achieve your goals.

As part of my action plan, I write down 5 actions I need to take daily that will lead me closer to my dream. I then list them in order of priority and intensity of action required. Whatever action that takes top priority on my list, that will be my focus. It will be the action I will focus on for that day. Everything else can wait.

These three steps have helped me achieve more than I have with any other goal setting process. Adapted from a system I learned from Brian Tracy's time management program. My system works for me, and I always advocate that you find something that works for you as well.

Define your impossible. Plan it and take massive action. Small actions produce big results.

THREE: Qualify Your Resources

I read a tweet the other day, and it said something like, "Why do people apply for jobs they clearly do not qualify for." And I thought to myself, "How limiting is that kind of thinking."

I've had many experiences where I was either over experienced and under qualified. And in some situations, I was over qualified and under experienced. Whatever the criteria will be for your selection, you are the only one that knows your potential.

Anyone that cannot qualify themselves with their own potential and possibility has no business starting the impossible. You, and only you can tap into your potential.

Some people may be able to identify it, and others will simply ignore it because it does not fit into their definition of true and real potential. You'll have to learn to rise above their ignorance.

Walt Disney was said not to be imaginative enough and so he did not qualify according to his employer. Some of the most successful people in the world are college dropouts and by any definition they do not qualify to those whose criteria is academic attendance and college degrees.

You don't need the permission of others to know you are good enough for the task at hand. What are your valuable and invaluable skills and abilities? What do you have to offer the world that no one else can?

Successful people are not only skilled and talented. What makes them unique is their passion for the skills and talents they have. They have what I call a skill of passion.

Not everyone has passion, but they may have a skill or a talent that comes naturally or learned through training. A skill of passion is what you will need to start your impossible.

> # ... YOU HAVE TO BELIEVE IN YOURSELF.

Passion allows you to do what you do out of deep love. And passion enables you to do much more and much better than you would with just skill or talent. Your passion is what sets you apart. Identify your skill of passion. Apply yourself to improving your ability to express your skill or talent. It may mean you have to go back to school or college.

However, with the world connected through the world wide web, improving your skill of passion may be in the comfort of your home, at your own pace and time.

You can learn from YouTube videos, webinars and seminars; workshops and many other educational tools. The assistant of a coach or mentor may also prove valuable to help you improve through practice.

What sets you apart from your peers is desire, design

and determination in relation to your skill of passion. Your learning is not only about passing a test or exam but learning a real-life skill you intend to use.

A destitute Steve Jobs attended calligraphy classes at Reeds college. The skill he learned from a class that was not even part of his curriculum is said to be largely responsible for the seismic shift in computing typeface and digital typography. Simply because he was more passionate about humanizing the computer experience.

The skills you learn from passion are more valuable to your resource pool because they are not based on you trying to qualifying on other people's terms. They are driven by your desire to want to learn a particular skill you are passionate about.

These skills or talents you will need, because they are what separates you from your peers. They are what makes you valuable to any relationship where you are a partner. But it takes unwavering faith in your abilities and talents to see beyond "Why do people apply for jobs they do not qualify for?"

You'll need to believe in yourself if anyone else is ever going to believe in you.

FOUR: Step up and take MASSIVE Action

'Go big or go home' is the famous saying used to ignite the flames of passion and fury for those that dare to reach for the stars. It's what we say in the business world. If you want to be a business person - buy a franchise. If you want to be an entrepreneur - reinvent the wheel, create the franchise.

Talk is overrated if it does not lead to action. And action is just as overrated if it is not massive enough to make a difference. I have five simple rules that guide my actions. Many other successful people have used these rules to great success.

A: Start Early. Make it a habit to wake up early. They say it's the early bird that gets the fattest worm. And there is so much truth to that.

Warren Buffet, the oracle of Omaha and the most successful investor of all time, is known to be up as early as 4am every day to get the most important tasks done. By the time the rest of the world gets up to work, he's out playing – expressing his skill of passion.

B: Work harder than you did you did yesterday. Your failure does not define you, your determination does.

Aristotle said, 'Pleasure in the job puts perfection in the work.' It's not hard labor but hard work that expresses determination in achieving the impossible.

A real decision is measured by the fact that you've taken a new action. If there's no hard work in your action, you haven't truly decided. Success is a choice. Your action is the result of that choice.

C: Never go more than three days without exercise. Your health is your wealth. If you are not healthy enough to produce, you won't be wealthy enough to enjoy the fruits of your labor.

You don't have to join the gym, but a decent amount of exercise is required if you are going to survive your failures to see through your successes.

Go jogging for 15 to 20 minutes a day. Walk a mile or

two, and gradually increase to more regular and longer sessions. Whatever decent amount of exercise you take on, commit to not going more than three days without it.

D: Make time to read every single day. Life is all about learning new things. If you stop learning, your growth becomes stagnant.

Human beings are wired to learn and change, not to stay in one place, doing the same thing over and over again.

...FOR OTHERS TO BELIEVE IN YOU

Reading is exercise for the mind. Reading opens you up to new ideas, concepts and experiences from people with valuable skills and knowledge.

However, don't read the same kind of books. Alternate between fiction and non-fiction, academic reference and historical memoirs.

E: Do one thing every day that gets you closer to your dream. Without seeming like I am repeating myself, "A journey of a thousand miles begins with a single step" a common saying that originated from a famous Chinese proverb and sometimes ascribed to the great Confucius.

One action everyday will get you closer to your impossible than if you waited for the right time or the right place to take the right amount of action.

They say it's the crazy ones who take action.

When other people look at them, they see abnormal. But to them normal is the new crazy. Because they are crazy enough to think they can change the world. For that reason, they normally do, by doing the common thing uncommonly well.

Don't be afraid to start, and start your impossible, because like me:

You are blessed with financial success and prosperity.

Anything you set your mind to, you will do.

You find it easy to make money, because,

You are Happy, you are Wealthy, and you are Prosperous.

More than anything

You are successful beyond measure.

Start Now
Star With Pain
Start With Fear
Start With Doubt
Start Where You Are
Start With Hands Shaking
Start With Your Voice Trembling
JUST START

So go out there and
#StartYourImpossible

Believe you can, and you are half way there.

Act as though it were impossible to fail...

| ABOUT THE AU- THOR

Vukani Nxumalo is the thinking entrepreneur. Passionate about the success of others through his love for finding solutions that work in business. He is the founder and CEO of RedOystor Media. The Visionary behind the Oystor Group of Companies.

When he's not writing books and solving problems, you will see him on stage speaking his mind about the many possibilities of the future.

Connect with him on social media - facebook, Twitter and Instagram - @VukaniNxumalo.

...and your success is guaranteed.

BIBLIOG-RAPHY

1. Business Insider - 29 famous people who failed before they succeeded

   LINK: https://www.businessinsider.com/successful-people-who-failed-at-first-2015-7?IR=T

2. Wanderlust Worker - 12 Famous People Who Failed Before Succeeding

   LINK: https://www.wanderlustworker.com/12-famous-people-who-failed-before-succeeding

3. The Start of Happiness – 4 Reasons Why you need to fail in order to succeed.

   LINK: https://www.startofhappiness.com/4-reasons-need-fail-order-succeed

4. 7 Surprising Benefits of Failure

LINK: https://www.wisebread.com/7-surprising-benefits-of-failure

5. 10 Ultra-successful millionaire and billionaire college dropouts

LINK: https://www.cnbc.com/2017/05/10/10-ultra-successful-millionaire-and-billionaire-college-dropouts

6. Rohn: How to bounce back from failure

LINK: https://www.success.com/rohn-how-to-bounce-back-from-failure

7. Before they were famous: Unglamorous First Jobs of Successful People.

LINK: http://www.fundera.com/blog/before-they-were-famous

8. Steve Jobs: the godfather of fonts as we know them.

LINK: http://www.digitaltrends.com/steve-jobs-the-godfather-of-fonts-as-we-know-them

BOOKS:

9. How successful people think - John C Maxwell
10. Rich dad Poor dad - Robert Kiyosaki
11. The Secret - Rhonda Byrne
12. The Power of Habit - Charles Duhigg
13. The Law of Success - Napoleon Hill
14. The Science of Getting Rich - Wallace D Wattles
15. Fail Forward: Turning Mistakes into Stepping Stones of Success - John C. Maxwell

16. Why A students work for C students - Robert Kiyosaki
17. Essentialism: The Disciplined Pursuit of Less - Greg McKeown
18. The Magic of Thinking BIG - David J. Schwartz
19. The Success Principles - Jack Canfield
20. The One Thing - Gary W. Keller & Jay Papasan
21. Focus: The Hidden Driver of Excellence - Daniel Goleman
22. The Value of Failure - Shane Lester
23. Deep Work - Cal Newport
24. Eat that frog - Brain Tracy
25. Stupid things young people say and do - Moss Mashamaite
26. Deep Work: Rules for Focused Success in a Distracted World - Cal Newport
27. Built to Last - James C. Collins & Jerry I. Porras
28. The Journey of a Thousand Miles Begins with a Single Step. Lao Tzu
29. Think and Grow Rich - Napoleon Hill
30. Intelligence, Information, Thinking - Edward de Bono
31. Adapt: Why Success Always Starts with Failure - Tim Harford
32. How to Fail at Almost Everything and Still Win Big: Kind of the Story of My Life - Scott Adams

redOystor

AN INVITATION FROM THE PUBLISHER

Join us at www.redoystor.com or connect with us on facebook and twitter @redOystor to be part of a community of people who love the very best in books and reading.

Whether you want to discover more about the author or the book, read more about upcoming events, interviews or watch trailers, or have a chance to win early limited editions, we think you will like what you are looking for.

And if you don't, let us know what's missing through our contact us page or email us at **theEditor@redoystor.com**

We love what we do, and we'd love you to be a part of it.

www.redoystor.com